TECHNICAL REPORT

No More Rights Without Remedies

An Impact Evaluation of the
National Crime Victim Law Institute's
Victims' Rights Clinics

Robert C. Davis • James M. Anderson • Susan Howley • Carol Dorris • Julie Whitman

Sponsored by the National Institute of Justice

RAND Safety and Justice Program

This project was sponsored by the National Institute of Justice and was conducted in the Safety and Justice Program of RAND Justice, Infrastructure, and Environment. The project was supported by Award No. 2007-VF-GX-0004, awarded by the National Institute of Justice, Office of Justice Programs, U.S. Department of Justice. The opinions, findings, and conclusions or recommendations expressed in this publication are those of the authors and do not necessarily reflect those of the Department of Justice.

Library of Congress Cataloging-in-Publication Data

Davis, Robert C. (Robert Carl)
  No more rights without remedies : an impact evaluation of the National Crime Victim Law Institute's victims' rights clinics / Robert C. Davis [and four others].
    pages cm
  Includes bibliographical references.
  ISBN 978-0-8330-7866-7 (pbk. : alk. paper)
  1. Victims of crimes—Legal status, laws, etc.—United States. 2. Criminal justice, Administration of—United States. 3. Privacy, Right of—United States. I. Securing rights for victims. II. Title.

  KF9763.D38 2012
  362.88'1560973—dc23

                                                                    2012050177

The RAND Corporation is a nonprofit institution that helps improve policy and decisionmaking through research and analysis. RAND's publications do not necessarily reflect the opinions of its research clients and sponsors.

RAND® is a registered trademark.

Published 2012 by the RAND Corporation
1776 Main Street, P.O. Box 2138, Santa Monica, CA 90407-2138
1200 South Hayes Street, Arlington, VA 22202-5050
4570 Fifth Avenue, Suite 600, Pittsburgh, PA 15213-2665
RAND URL: http://www.rand.org/
To order RAND documents or to obtain additional information, contact
Distribution Services: Telephone: (310) 451-7002;
Fax: (310) 451-6915; Email: order@rand.org

Preface

This is the second of two reports evaluating the National Crime Victim Law Institute's victims' rights clinics. The evaluation was funded by the National Institute of Justice (award 2007-VF-GX-0004). The clinics were designed to increase awareness of victims' rights among criminal justice professionals and to respond to violations of rights through legal advocacy. The first report, *Securing Rights for Victims: A Process Evaluation of the National Crime Victim Law Institute's Victims' Rights Clinics* (Davis et al., 2009b), included case studies of the individual state clinics. It synthesized commonalities of experiences among the individual clinics, as well as differences in their approaches and environments. The current report examines the clinics' impact on the expansion of rights for victims, on court officials' attitudes toward victims' rights, on the extent to which victims' rights are honored in the criminal disposition process, and on the treatment of victims' rights in the print media. It also includes a discussion of sustainability of the clinics. Both reports are intended for an audience of researchers and criminal justice practitioners interested in victims' rights.

This research was conducted under the auspices of the RAND Safety and Justice Program, part of RAND Justice, Infrastructure, and Environment (JIE), a division of the RAND Corporation dedicated to improving policy and decisionmaking in a wide range of policy domains, including civil and criminal justice, infrastructure protection and homeland security, transportation and energy policy, and environmental and natural resource policy.

Questions or comments about this report should be sent to the project leader, Robert C. Davis (Robert_Davis@rand.org). For more information on the Safety and Justice Program, see http://www.rand.org/jie/research/safety-justice.html or contact the director at sj@rand.org.

Contents

Figures

Tables

Summary

The National Crime Victim Law Institute (NCVLI) victims' rights clinics are an effort to remedy what many perceived as a serious deficit in victims' rights legislation. Although all states have laws protecting victims' rights and many have constitutional amendments establishing rights for victims, the rights of many victims still are not honored or observed. In large measure, this may be because there are no remedies enforceable when victims are denied their rights. The NCVLI clinics were intended to promote awareness, education, and enforcement of crime victims' rights in the criminal justice system. The victims' rights clinics sought to protect and enforce rights for victims in the court process through filing motions in criminal cases in which victims' rights were denied and by seeking appellate decisions that interpreted and reinforced victims' rights statutes. By providing direct representation to individual victims in criminal court, NCVLI hoped not only to increase the observance of rights in those particular cases but also to increase awareness of victims' rights by prosecutors, judges, and police officers in general.

Assessing the impact of the NCVLI clinics is a difficult task in part because the clinics have two distinct foci: to alter the "legal landscape" with respect to victims' rights and to promote the rights of victims in individual cases. To try to capture the scope of clinic activities, the impact evaluation employed multiple methods. We sought to determine how clinic representation affected the exercise of rights in individual cases in several ways. First, we compared prosecutor case files in which victims were represented by clinic attorneys and similar cases in which victims did not have representation, for indications of how victims' rights were addressed. Second, we surveyed victims in the two samples of cases to elicit their perspectives on whether their rights were observed and on their satisfaction with the justice process. We surveyed prosecutors, judges, victim advocates, and defense attorneys to ascertain their opinions about victims' rights and about the NCVLI clinics. We examined legislation and court rules pertaining to victims' rights before and after the start of the clinics. We also examined appellate decisions relating to victims' rights pre- and postclinic. We examined the treatment of victims' rights in the print media pre- and postclinic. Finally, we interviewed victims' rights clinic directors to obtain and synthesize their thoughts on sustainability of the clinics.

Key findings from the evaluation include the following:

- Survey results indicated a shift toward more-favorable attitudes toward victims' rights and greater compliance with victims' rights by court officials after establishment of the clinics. The changes were small with respect to attitudes toward victims' rights but larger with respect to perceptions of compliance with victims' rights.

- In our analysis of prosecutor case files, we found differences in compliance on some measures in some jurisdictions between cases in which victims were represented by attorneys and those in which they were not. In the aggregate, however, the analysis of prosecutor files did not suggest an increase in compliance as a result of having a victims' rights attorney.
- According to our surveys of victims from the prosecutor case-file sample, victims represented by clinic attorneys more often reported that they were notified of defendants' release from jail, that they had made a victim-impact statement, that they were notified of the case disposition, and that they were referred to counseling services. However, victims represented by clinic attorneys were also *less* satisfied with the way they were treated by court officials, *less* satisfied with the court process, and *less* satisfied with the outcomes of their cases.
- We found some, but inconsistent, evidence that clinics made a difference in the expansion of victims' rights both in terms of legislation related to victims' rights and in terms of appellate decisions.
- We did not find a consistent increase in the number of articles in the print media about victims' rights, nor did we observe a change in the proportion of articles sympathetic to victims' rights.

The results of the impact evaluation indicate that victims' rights clinics can make a difference in promoting the rights of victims in individual cases; they may help more generally to promote a more sympathetic view of victims' rights among court officials; and they have had some influence in expanding the rights of victims in the states where they reside through their involvement in influential appellate decisions and legislative efforts. After assessing the information we gathered during the course of the process evaluation, we believe that the victims' rights clinics have been somewhat successful in achieving their key goals. However, funding remains a problem for the clinics, and the current economic climate makes it unlikely that the demonstration clinics can be replicated on a large scale, using the current model.

Abbreviations

DA	district attorney
M	mean
NCVC	National Center for Victims of Crime
NCVLI	National Crime Victim Law Institute
NIJ	National Institute of Justice
OVC	Office for Victims of Crime
PIMS	Prosecutor Information Management System
SD	standard deviation
VINE	Victim Information and Notification Everyday
VIS	victim-impact statement
VOCA	Victims of Crime Act
VRA	victims' rights amendment

CHAPTER ONE

Introduction

Once considered only witnesses to the state's case, victims have increasingly been recognized in statutes as having rights in the criminal disposition process. But the rights that exist in statute seldom have effective remedies and therefore often have not been honored in practice. Kilpatrick and Otto (1987), writing about victims' rights, noted,

> Legislators should be careful . . . to [e]nsure that any rights conferred are real, that is, the victim has an avenue of redress should those rights be denied. Providing rights without remedies would result in the worst of consequences, such as feelings of helplessness, lack of control, and further victimization. (pp. 26–27)

The National Crime Victim Law Institute (NCVLI), with funding from the U.S. Department of Justice Office for Victims of Crime (OVC), established a demonstration project that provides attorneys to advocate for the rights of individual victims and establish a body of case law that expands the rights for victims generally. The demonstration project clinics aim to make the rights that victims have in statute a reality in the courtroom.

A Brief History of Victims' Rights

The legal rights of crime victims have been significantly expanded in the past 30 years. During this time, multiple pieces of legislation at the federal and state levels have begun to provide victims with rights to be informed, heard, and protected throughout the criminal justice process. Although the landscape of victims' rights has advanced considerably at the legislative level, the criminal justice system has been slow to adapt the adjudicative process to incorporate the rights and concerns of crime victims. To provide some perspective about current issues facing the recognition and enforcement of victims' rights, we provide a brief history of victims' traditional place in the legal system and the legislative changes that have begun to alter the legal landscape of victims' rights (for a more complete review, see Davis et al., 2009a).

During colonial times, victims of crime were an important component of criminal justice, often paying the sheriff to pursue the defendant and hiring the prosecutor. However, as the American criminal justice system evolved to one of public prosecution, with the prosecutor representing the interest of the state, crime victims were relegated to a marginal role in the prosecutions of their offenders (Eikenberry, 1987). The lack of victim participation in the criminal justice system was largely due to the fundamental view that a crime was an offense against society rather than against an individual. This belief led to structuring the U.S. criminal justice system to rely on publicly funded police officers and prosecutors to seek justice and retribution for crimes (O'Hara, 2005). Because the system focused on righting wrongs against society rather than the victim, crime victims typically only served as case witnesses and often did not possess rights to further participate in the prosecutorial process or receive restitution for their individual harms. The result was a two-party adversarial system that was not structured to consider the opinions or needs of the victims. The rights of individual victims began to receive attention in the 1960s and 1970s, when advocates raised awareness about the justice system's mistreatment of victims and challenged deeply ingrained views about victims' place in the criminal justice process (Davis and Mulford, 2008).

Spurred by these social justice movements, in the 1980s, significant pieces of legislation were passed in many states that began to provide rights to crime victims. A major force for legislative change came from recommendations contained in a 1982 report by the President's Task Force on Victims of Crime. In the report, the task force advocated balancing criminal defendants' rights with the rights of victims and recommended that efforts be made to increase victims' participation in the criminal justice process. The task force also called for procedures to provide victims with restitution for crime-related financial losses. Around this same time, Congress enacted several pieces of legislation providing certain rights to crime victims, including the right to receive restitution and the right to submit victim-impact statements prior to sentencing hearings (Victim and Witness Protection Act of 1982, Pub. L. 97-291; Victims of Crime Act [VOCA] of 1984, Pub. L. 98-473). Since then, Congress has continued to pass legislation that expands victims' rights and roles within the criminal justice process (Victims' Rights and Restitution Act of 1990, Pub. L. 101-647; Violent Crime Control and Law Enforcement Act of 1994, Pub. L. 103-322; Crime Victims' Rights Act of 2004, Pub. L. 108-405). Concurrent with legislative changes at the federal level, states began enacting legislation providing rights to crime victims, who previously had little to no guaranteed rights, to participate in the criminal justice process. Today, all 50 states have passed some form of victims' rights legislation, and 32 states have adopted constitutional amendments guaranteeing victims certain rights (O'Hara, 2005).

These pieces of legislation recognized the concept of victims' rights as an issue that is of importance throughout the entire criminal justice process and have begun to address victims' rights across several broad categories (Beloof, 2007; Howley and Dorris, 2007). One of victims' most basic rights involves the right to be notified—to be informed of the rights and services they are entitled to receive, to be notified of case-relevant court proceedings, and to be notified of the status of their offenders, including notification of an offender's escape or release from custody. Without notification, victims would be unable to assert most of the additional rights they have been afforded. This includes the right to be present at case-relevant criminal justice proceedings, ranging from pretrial hearings to postconviction sentencing and parole hearings. Another right highly valued by victims is the right to be heard. This right involves the ability to confer with criminal justice officials who are making decisions about the resolution of the case, including prosecutorial decisions to press charges and offer plea bargains. Should the case proceed to sentencing, victims' rights to be heard extend to providing oral or written victim-impact statements about the harms that resulted from the crime committed against them. A critical victims' right is protection from harm and, to the extent possible, of victims' privacy. These rights include protection from defendant contact or intimidation, protection while attending court proceedings, and protection from adverse consequences from employers for missing work to attend case-related activities. Finally, victims' right to restitution involves restoring the victim to the financial state in which he or she would have been had the crime not been committed. Receiving restitution rights often involves defendant payment for victims' costs associated with physical injury, mental injury, lost wages, or lost property (Beloof, 2007; Howley and Dorris, 2007).

Despite substantial progress made in the federal and state legislatures toward providing crime victims with rights, significant gaps remain. Most states' victims' rights legislation does not address the full gamut of victims' rights issues. In addition, most states limit the types of crimes and victims who are eligible to receive rights. Only about 40 percent of states guarantee rights to all victims of all crimes (Howley and Dorris, 2007). All states do provide some victims the right to receive restitution, be notified of court appearances, and submit a victim-impact statement prior to sentencing hearings (Beloof, 2003; Cassell, 2005; Davis and Mulford, 2008). Many states provide victims with additional rights—for example, the right to consult with prosecutors or judges before plea-bargaining decisions, the right to be present at trial, the right to receive protection during trial, or the right to be heard at parole hearings (Howley and Dorris, 2007; Johnson and Morgan, 2008; Kelly and Erez, 1997; Ruback and Thompson, 2001). The extent of victims' involvement with activities made possible by each of these rights, however, varies by state. For example, in some states, a victim are simply informed by the prosecutor that his or her case will be resolved via plea bargain, while victims in other states are allowed to offer their views or consult with the prosecutor during the negotiation process. Finally, although all states have afforded some victims at least some rights, many states do not have mechanisms in place for victims to enforce those rights or seek redress when these rights are violated (Beloof, 2005).

Research has also found that the criminal justice system often fails to comply with the requirements of victims' rights legislation. One survey funded by the National Institute of Justice (NIJ) found that, even in states with strong victims' rights legislation, victims often were not notified of hearings, were denied the right to be heard, or failed to receive restitution (Kirkpatrick, Beatty, and Howley, 1998). More recently, the U.S. General Accounting Office (2004) reported that the government was collecting only 4 percent of criminal debt, including restitution, and that 70 percent of that uncollected debt was money owed to victims. Studies examining victims' rights compliance within specific states have similarly found that victims are often denied their rights or not even notified of their rights and that systems for ensuring compliance are unsatisfactory (Fritsch et al., 2004; Regional Research Institute for Human Services, 2003; Office of the Auditor General of Florida, 2001). Research examining attitudes of court officials has found that, although officials often rate victims' rights as important, they also believe that the role of victims in the process should be limited (Englebrecht, 2011). Other research has similarly found that victims often report feeling as though they have no real control during the process and that their rights are not taken seriously (Bibas, 2006).

The National Crime Victim Law Institute's State and Federal Clinics and System Demonstration Project

Recognizing the need for legal advocacy to further the protection of victims and the progression of victims' rights (Beloof, 2007), in 2000, NCVLI was established to be a national resource for crime victims and their attorneys. NCVLI's overall mission is to promote "balance and fairness in the justice system through crime victim centered legal advocacy, education, and resource sharing" (NCVLI, undated). NCVLI carries out its mission through a variety of activities, including hosting conferences and training programs to educate criminal justice officials; conducting and promoting further victim-impact legislation; litigating to enforce victims' rights; and providing technical assistance to victims' attorneys.

In 2002, NCVLI furthered its mission when it received support from OVC in the Office of Justice Programs of the U.S. Department of Justice to create the State and Federal Clinics and System Demonstration Project, which ended in 2009. A key component of this project was the establishment of pro bono victims' rights clinics in several states across the country. By 2005, eight state clinics had been established in Arizona (two there), Maryland, New Mexico, South Carolina, Idaho, New Jersey, and Utah. During the demonstration project, Arizona was selected to additionally handle work in the federal courts. The purpose of the demonstration project was to test the viability of operating legal clinics that could successfully protect and enforce local victims' rights. To identify particularly successful models, the clinics were all tasked with implementing NCVLI's mission and goals, but they were allowed leeway in how they chose to operate their clinics and carry out their work (NCVLI, 2009).

Overall, NCVLI envisioned that the clinics' work would increase criminal justice officials' acceptance of victims' rights and, subsequently, officials' observance of victims' rights within the courts. These goals would be carried out by the state clinics in several ways. First, the clinics' attorneys would work toward ensuring rights for the individual victims they served. In doing so, NCVLI hoped that attorney representation of individual victims would not only aid those individual victims but also have a more widespread impact on criminal justice officials and the courts. Successful representation of clients in these cases would establish precedent for recognizing victims' rights in future cases. Additionally, the presence of the victims' attorneys in these cases would increase local court officials' acceptance of victims' rights, which would extend to cases in which victims were not represented by clinic attorneys. Second, NCVLI hoped that each clinic would selectively bring forth cases at the appellate level, pushing judges to expand or clarify victims' rights through written decisions. Well-argued appeals had the potential to benefit victims' rights in one of two ways. Favorable decisions would establish precedent for future cases in which victims' rights were at issue. Unfavorable rulings could be used to make the case for expansion or clarification of victims' rights and subsequently partner with advocacy groups to push for change in the legislative arena.

NCVLI envisioned that the clinics would employ several common strategies for operating the clinics. First, NCVLI encouraged the clinics to use the services of pro bono attorneys and law students as much as possible. There were several reasons behind NCVLI's desire to make use of these individuals. First, pro bono attorneys and law students would reduce initial operating costs, and, if a sufficient pool of pro bono attorneys and law students could be cultivated, the work of the clinic could continue to be carried out beyond the support of the demonstration project. Second, NCVLI hoped that the working with the clinic would increase these individuals' advocacy for victims' rights in their current or future legal professions. To change attitudes toward victims' rights, the clinics were also instructed to conduct outreach efforts, including ongoing training programs with criminal justice professionals and law students and programs to inform members of the community about victims' rights. These interactions were intended to educate current and future criminal justice officials about victims' rights and increase acceptance of the clinics' work within the local community and legal system (NCVLI, 2009).

As a first step, all clinics pushed for victims' standing to enforce their rights within their jurisdictions. Standing is a legal doctrine that allows or disallows a party to intervene in a legal proceeding. Without standing, victims and victims' rights clinics have no right to intervene in legal proceedings. As previously mentioned, most states do not have mechanisms in place for victims to enforce their rights or seek redress when their rights are violated (Howley and Dorris, 2007). This is because states vary in whether they expressly allow victims standing to assert their rights in trial courts or to seek appellate decisions (Beloof, 2005).

Traditionally, there has been significant resistance on the part of criminal justice officials and the courts to grant victims standing to assert their rights. Prosecutors, judges, and defense counsel have expressed concern that allowing standing would provide victims with too much control over case outcomes and might infringe on defendants' guaranteed rights. The clinics hoped to change officials' attitudes on victim standing.

In addition, the legal system has been slow to adapt to victims' rights legislation, and, as a result, the legal process is often not set up to effectively recognize victims' rights. For example, the window of time in which a victims' rights issue is deemed relevant by the courts can be fairly small. In order to even be considered, a victims' rights request must be presented to the court at the proper procedural stage: too soon and the court can rule the issue not yet ripe, too late and the court can deem the issue moot (Beloof, 2005). Therefore, clinic attorneys would need to devise strategies to begin to change the legal systems' procedures to allow for victim participation. Finally, all clinics would need to consider victims' current standing in trial and appellate courts. If a particular jurisdiction did not explicitly grant victims standing, then that clinic's attorneys would need to weigh the risks of pushing for standing and receiving an unfavorable decision against the benefits of gaining precedent for standing with a favorable decision.

In practice, the clinics also were given some freedom to structure and operate themselves as they saw fit. Many of the resulting differences in clinics' structure and operation were based on the location, local legal climate, and resources available to a particular clinic. One of the primary differences between clinics was the organizational model under which the clinics chose to operate. Some of the clinics operated within a larger victim services agency that was already serving a variety of other victim needs. Other clinics were established within law schools and primarily relied on second- or third-year law-student volunteers to operate the clinic. Finally, some clinics operated as stand-alone entities, without the support of an agency or law school (NCVLI, 2009).

Each of these organization models was associated with both benefits and drawbacks, which, in turn, had implications for how each clinic carried out its work. For example, different organizational models influenced the extent to which a clinic was able to rely on pro bono attorneys and law students and the extent to which it was able to provide comprehensive victim services to its clients. In addition, clinics that were not affiliated with more-established institutions or agencies often needed to expend more resources on outreach efforts, including efforts to secure clients and to establish amicable relationships with local criminal justice officials. Finally, differences in clinic structure often dictated how attorneys approached representation of their clients. Some clinics often attempted to revolve clients' issues through backdoor conversations with criminal justice officials. Clinics with less well-established relationships preferred to assert their clients' rights by moving directly into litigation. In sum, although all the clinics were working toward the same goals, there was a significant degree of variability in how the clinics operated and how they prioritized clinic activities (NCVLI, 2009).

Evaluation of Demonstration Clinics

The RAND Corporation and the National Center for Victims of Crime (NCVC) conducted a two-part evaluation of NCVLI's state and federal victims' rights clinics. The first stage of this study consisted of a process evaluation of all eight victims' rights clinics to examine how the clinics have been implemented, problems they have had to overcome, and how different clinic models affect the work they do. We completed our process evaluation in 2009 and began work on the second part of this research and the focus of this report, an evaluation of the impact that the clinics have had on changing criminal justice officials' acceptance and observance of victims' rights. We first provide a brief summary of our findings from the earlier process evaluation (Davis et al., 2009a) before turning to the impact evaluation.

Process Evaluation

During our process evaluation of the demonstration clinics, we conducted site visits to all eight demonstration clinics to gather data from a variety of sources. We interviewed directors and clinic staff to learn about how each clinic operated (e.g., staffing, sources of client recruitment, distribution of clinic information), the clinic's activities (e.g., training of criminal justice officials, trial and appellate court work), and clinic staff perceptions of the clinics' impact on criminal justice officials' attitudes and behavior. To gather information about victims' experiences in working with the clinic, we conducted focus groups with a sample of each clinic's clients. We also interviewed criminal justice personnel (e.g., judges, prosecutors, defense attorneys, victim advocates) to understand how criminal justice officials viewed the work of the clinics and how the clinics' work had changed the way victims were treated during the criminal justice process. Finally, clinic staff provided us with statistics from cases opened within the previous year (e.g., type of case, location of case, referral sources, victims' rights issues that brought the case to their attention, clinic actions to aid client).

The process evaluation provided insights into the clinics' work. Overall, the clinics' work was in alignment with NCVLI's goals and objectives. All the clinics were representing victims and pushing officials in the legal system to recognize their clients' rights. Five of the clinics had also worked on appellate cases, thereby playing a role in changing the legal landscape of victims' rights or, in the case of unfavorable appellate decisions, highlighting the need for further clarification of current victims' rights legislation. During our focus groups, victim clients were extremely complimentary of the assistance they had received and highly praised the clinics' work. All the clinics interacted with criminal justice officials both as representatives of their clients and through educational programs to change officials' attitudes and increase acceptance of victims' rights.

The clinics also reported encountering some difficulties along the way. Because attorney representation of victims was a relatively new concept, many sites reported resistance to change on the part of local court officials, although the level of resistance varied depending on the clinics' prior standing within the local legal system. Some clinics attempted to overcome this resistance by highlighting ways in which the clinic's involvement could help court officials (e.g., filing motions, gathering case paperwork). Most clinic staff reported that, with time, distrust of the clinics by court officials had diminished. Many clinics also reported difficulty retaining staff and finding attorneys experienced enough with victims' rights issues to be of service. This issue was particularly problematic for clinics that were receiving more referrals for cases than they could handle. Other clinics less well connected to the community reported the opposite problem: low case loads. These clinics worked to increase their case loads through outreach programs and by reaching out to victims in high-profile cases featured in the media. Finally, most clinics reported difficulties with securing continuous funding to support their work. Federal funding to operate the clinics was not always secure from year to year, and, although most clinics had applied for supplemental state grants, acquiring additional funding was difficult. Some clinics were beginning to seek out more-innovative sources of funding, such as corporate donors to subsidize office space.

Impact Evaluation of Selected National Crime Victim Law Institute Clinics

The current report describes the second phase of this research, an examination of the impact that selected clinics have had on changing the legal culture with regard to victims' rights. This impact study was conducted for several reasons. First, although the process evaluation found that the clinics were pushing to improve and expand the legal system's recognition of their clients' rights, a true test of the clinics' success would come by examining whether the clinics had actually changed criminal justice officials' acceptance and observance of victims' rights. Furthermore, our interviews with small samples of criminal justice officials and victims was a suitable method to gain insight into clinic operations, but, to truly understand how the clinics had affected acceptance of victims' rights by the criminal justice system, we needed to survey a larger sample of both victims and criminal justice officials. Finally, our process evaluation found that these clinics' operations differed along a variety of dimensions (e.g., business models, use of pro bono attorneys, standing within the criminal justice community). Because the concept of pro bono victims' clinics is, to a certain extent, in its developmental stages, an impact evaluation was necessary to provide some insight into how the setup of victims' clinics influences their impact on the criminal justice system.

We encountered several challenges associated with conducting the impact evaluation. First, although each of the clinics was working under the broad umbrella of enforcing and expanding victims' rights, the specific goals of each clinic program were quite different in nature. Evaluating a program with such varied goals—including victim advocacy, educating criminal justice officials, connecting victims with services, and changing the legal landscape through appellate decisions, court rulings, and statutes—presented challenges for measuring the overall success of each program. Although we included measures of each goal in our evaluation, it is difficult to conclude the extent to which each goal contributes to the overall success of the clinic. Is a clinic that has had some success with changing the legal landscape of its jurisdiction through appellate decisions more successful than a clinic that has been able to represent a large number of individual victims or a clinic that has increased criminal justice officials' compliance with rights that currently exist in the local jurisdiction? As previously mentioned, clinics operated under different organizational models and in different legal climates, which had some influence on the way that the clinics were able to carry out their work. It would be difficult for a clinic to be able to fully prioritize each of activities with which it was tasked.

There were also challenges in measuring the success of specific program goals. One such challenge was measuring the impact that the clinics had on changing the legal landscape of victims' rights in their jurisdictions. It is difficult to measure the extent to which clinics changed the legal culture of a local area when just one major appellate decision can produce such a large shift in the effort to expand victims' rights. In order to provide some insight into the clinics' impact, we would need to quantify the effect that judicial rulings had on various aspects of victims' rights, as well as the long-term implications of these rulings.

Finally, we encountered challenges measuring the extent to which the clinics had changed criminal justice officials' attitudes toward victims' rights. At the time that this impact evaluation was conceived, most clinics had been in operation for some time. Because these clinics were already working within the local legal system, it would be difficult to gather accurate baseline data from criminal justice officials about their opinions of victims' rights before the clinic was established. Individuals may not be aware of or be able to accurately remember the extent to which their attitudes have changed over time, making reliance on retrospective reports problematic. These challenges and our approaches to addressing them are further discussed in the body of this report.

CHAPTER TWO

Method

As the introduction noted, the purpose of the victims' rights clinics is to advance victims' rights through education, litigation, and direct representation of victims in individual criminal cases. Table 2.1 sets out more specifically our understanding of the goals of the NCVLI clinics. These include

- assist in enforcing rights for individual victims and getting them help for crime-related needs, thereby increasing satisfaction of victims with the justice process
- change attitudes of criminal justice officials toward victims' rights and increase their knowledge about rights
- change the legal landscape: establish victim standing and develop positive case law
- increase compliance of criminal justice officials with victims' rights
- sustain the clinic through developing alternative sources of funding.

This list was developed through consultation with a variety of sources, including NIJ's evaluation solicitation and the grant proposals of the individual clinics to NCVLI. In addition, we discussed clinic goals with clinic staff during site visits. The preliminary list was vetted with NIJ and OVC staff and finally with the director of NCVLI.

The right-hand column of Table 2.1 details the methods that we used to gauge the success of the clinics in attaining each goal. To assess clinic effects on increasing victims' satisfaction with the criminal justice process through actions to ensure that rights are enforced, we conducted surveys with two groups of victims: one sample of victims represented by clinic attorneys and another sample of victims who had no representation. We used the same victim surveys to determine whether clinic assessments of social service needs and referrals made a difference in terms of increasing contacts between victims and service programs.

We also used surveys to measure changes in attitudes and behavior of criminal justice officials toward victims' rights. We conducted comprehensive surveys of prosecutors, judges, prosecutor victim advocates, and public defenders through their statewide membership associations. In one state, where the victims' rights clinic had not yet begun taking cases, we conducted surveys pre- and post–clinic opening so that we could measure changes in attitudes over time. In other states where this was not feasible because clinics already existed, we conducted a single survey that asked respondents to gauge how much their attitudes had shifted since the clinic began operations. To gauge shifts in community opinion, we examined changes in the frequency and tone of victims' rights coverage in major print media before and after clinics opened their doors.

Table 2.1
Impact Assessment of Victims' Rights Clinics

Clinic Goals	Methods of Measurement
(1) Assist individual victims by (a) advocating for rights through representation in court and calls or inquiries on behalf of victims and (b) assessing social service needs and referring victims to clinicians and other service programs	Surveys of victims in clinic cases versus cases without clinic representation in order to assess the extent to which rights were observed, satisfaction with the justice process, and social service needs met
(2) Change knowledge, attitudes, and behavior of criminal justice officials and the larger community through trial court advocacy work, training, and presentations and distribution of information about the clinic through brochures, email blast websites, and newsletters	Surveys of judges, prosecutors, victim advocates, and public defenders either pre- and postclinic or retrospectively in those states where the clinic is well-established Media coverage of victims' rights stories before and after opening of the clinic
(3) Change legal landscape through filing appellate cases and amicus briefs and promoting legislative and court rule changes	Appellate decisions favorable to victims Changes to court rules Legislation in which clinic staff had a hand or that arose from clinic cases
(4) Increase compliance with victims' rights by criminal justice officials through all of the above activities	Victims' rights observed coded from prosecutor files, comparison of clinic cases, concurrent nonclinic cases, and archival preclinic cases
(5) Sustain clinic through developing proposals, meeting with potential funders, and developing innovative sources of financing	Level of funding Diversification from OVC funding

To determine the role that clinics have had in changing the legal landscape in their states, we updated work we included in the process evaluation report that identified and analyzed appellate decisions, court rules, and statutes favorable to victims' rights. We developed metrics to measure impact in this area and examined the role that clinic staff had in any victims' rights legislation passed since the clinic began.

The bottom-line objective for the clinics is increasing enforcement of criminal justice officials with victims' rights. To gauge compliance, we compared observance of victims' rights as recorded in three samples of prosecutor case files: (1) a sample of cases represented by a clinic attorney, (2) an archival sample of cases that pre-date the clinic, and (3) a sample of current cases in which victims were not represented by an attorney.

Finally, we examined progress that clinics have made in sustaining their activities through soliciting and developing sources of funding beyond OVC dollars. We assessed success in obtaining funds from state government and private sources, as well as innovative ways to generate revenue.

Choice of Clinics for the Impact Evaluation

Because NIJ specified that three of the eight NCVLI clinics were to be included in the impact evaluation, there were two potential strategies that we could have used in the selection process. One was to choose the clinics randomly. The advantage of this strategy is that the evaluation would be determining the impact of the "typical" or "average" clinic. The other strategy was to choose the clinics purposefully. We chose the latter strategy for two reasons: First, we thought it more useful to conduct an impact assessment of what victims' rights clinics at their best can achieve. By including those clinics that were more mature and had been able to implement and refine the ideal, we were, in a sense, testing NCVLI's model. We thought that this would yield more-useful information for policymakers than assessing the impact of clinics that might have implemented the model less well.

The other reason for purposeful selection of clinics is that we needed to ensure a large enough volume of cases so that samples of a sufficient size (which we estimated to be about 150 across all sites) could be constructed. The ability to generate a sufficiently large volume of cases in which victims are represented by attorneys was precluded in some sites by the small number of cases opened by the clinics there, by the geographic dispersion of cases across counties,[1] and by the relatively short time that clinics had been operating. Data collected for the process evaluation on the size of clinic case loads and geographic dispersion of cases indicated that the impact work should not include Idaho or New Mexico because of case loads that were too small for our purposes (see Figure 2.1). The New Jersey clinic had a large case load, but, because its case load was spread out, there was no single county or small group of counties that could generate a large number of cases. The Arizona clinic's case load was spread across federal, tribal, and state cases, reducing the number of cases comparable to the other clinics.

Given these restrictions, we determined that the best choices for the impact work were Utah, South Carolina, and Maryland. Together, these sites had opened about 300 cases since the clinics' inceptions within either two or three counties within their states (we estimated 180 for Utah in Salt Lake and Utah counties, 75 for Maryland in Baltimore and Prince George's counties, and 45 for South Carolina in Richland, Darlington, and Lexington counties).

These clinics made sense as subjects of the evaluation for other reasons as well. The Maryland clinic has done significant work on the appellate level, and its founder has been a strong force for legislative change in his state. But it is also true that the founder of the Maryland

Figure 2.1
Clinic Case Loads

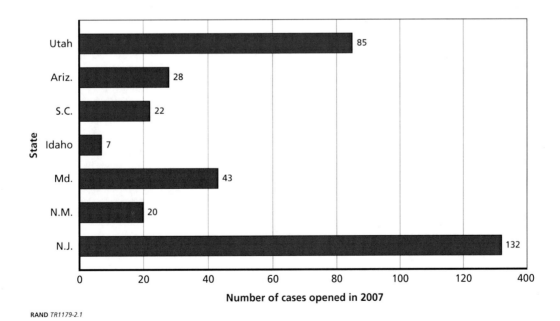

RAND *TR1179-2.1*

---

[1]   Clustering of cases within a few counties is important because we had to work out agreements with the prosecutor of each county that participated in the impact evaluation to give us access to files and contact information for victims.

clinic was very involved with the issue of victims' rights and representation long before NCVLI funded the clinic. For that reason, it would have been difficult at this point to demonstrate a sharp contrast with the preclinic period. Thus, it made sense to include two clinics in states where there was not such a strong history of victims' rights work by a clinic director. Utah and South Carolina fit that bill and represented interesting contrasts in approaches to their work: Utah's work is more based on litigation, while South Carolina took a less adversarial approach to trying to enforce victims' rights, conversing with prosecutors and police officials.

In addition to these three sites, when conducting surveys of criminal justice officials, we added Colorado to the set. Because the Colorado clinic was just getting under way, we had a unique opportunity to gather baseline survey data on attitudes of criminal justice officials at the beginning of the evaluation period and to compare those results with a second round of survey results obtained a year after the clinic started accepting clients. From a scientific perspective, this made it easier to measure the effect of the clinic.

In developing these choices, we were also guided by conversations we had with NIJ and OVC staff and the head of NCVLI. We believe that these choices—Maryland, Utah, South Carolina, and Colorado—represent the best chance to test the impact of the NCVLI legal clinic model.[2]

In conducting the evaluation, we counted heavily on clinic directors to help us gain the cooperation of local prosecutors and state prosecutor, judge, victim advocate, and public defender associations. The directors of the clinics each indicated that they were willing and capable of doing that job for us and, indeed, each was instrumental in gaining cooperation of local criminal justice agencies.

---

[2] NCVLI's director objected to the inclusion of the South Carolina clinic because it focused less on litigation than the other clinics did—one of the reasons that we felt it useful to include in the evaluation.

CHAPTER THREE

Survey of Criminal Justice Officials' Attitudes Toward and Knowledge of Victims' Rights

We conducted surveys of prosecutors, judges, victim advocates, and defense attorneys to determine whether they had changed their attitudes toward victims' rights since their local clinics opened their doors. The surveys were fielded in the three states in which we were evaluating a clinic: South Carolina, Maryland, and Utah. In addition, we also fielded a survey in Colorado, where the victims' rights clinic had not yet started to accept cases. Colorado offered us a unique opportunity to assess views of victims' rights both before and after a victims' rights clinic opened, unlike the other states, where we had to rely on retrospective information from respondents. The surveys were completed using web-based technology using the survey development tool QuestionPro, working through the state associations for each of the four groups of criminal justice officials. We asked the victims' rights clinic directors to introduce us to the heads of the state associations of prosecutors, judges, prosecutor victim advocates, public defenders, and the private bar. Working through the state associations, we sent the survey via email to the membership roster of each group. Initial mailings were followed up by two reminders.

Surveys in all sites were similarly worded. However, because the surveys in Utah, Maryland, and South Carolina were administered well after the launch of the clinics, questions were posed retrospectively. That is, respondents were asked to compare their present attitudes and behavior with respect to victims' rights with their attitudes and behavior prior to the date that the clinic opened. Because it depends on the sometimes-imperfect memory of the respondents, this is not an ideal methodology, but it was necessary for the clinics for which we could not collect baseline data.

In Colorado, the two administrations of the survey queried respondents about their current attitudes and behavior.

The surveys contained three sets of scaled items. One set asked respondents their opinions on victims' rights issues, with multiple-choice answers chosen from a five-point Likert scale. The second set asked about compliance with victims' rights statutes among prosecutors, judges, and defense attorneys. The final question set queried respondents about their knowledge of state victims' rights statutes through a series of multiple-choice items. The items for the three scales were authored by project researchers from NCVC.

The eight questions about respondents' opinions about victims' rights are as follows:

- Crime victims should have explicit rights in the criminal justice process.
- Crime victims should have legal standing to enforce their rights in court.
- Crime victims should have the option of having an attorney represent them in criminal court.

- There should be legal remedies for victims who are denied rights.
- Victims' rights often conflict with defendants' rights.
- My organization does not have sufficient staff to comply fully with victims' rights.
- Complying with victims' rights requirements frequently delays dispositions.
- Victims' rights attorneys can be helpful to me.

They range from questions about the appropriateness of rights to questions about perceived problems in implementing rights. Each item had the same five response options: strongly agree (1), agree (2), neutral (3), disagree (4), and strongly disagree (5).

The second set of questions asked respondents their thoughts on how reliably victims' rights statutes were followed by court officials, including prosecutors, judges, and defense attorneys. These four items used the same five-point Likert scale (strongly agree to strongly disagree) that the opinion questions used. The four items are as follows:

- Prosecutors in my jurisdiction comply with victims' rights requirements.
- Prosecutors in my jurisdiction are willing to argue in court for victims' rights to be honored.
- Defense attorneys in my jurisdiction accept crime victims' rights as written in law and do not actively oppose their exercise in the courtroom.
- Judges in my jurisdiction are aware of and uphold victims' rights.

In addition to these common items, the three-state surveys contained some unique questions not included on the Colorado survey. In particular, the three-state survey included questions about contact with clinic attorneys and whether the clinic attorneys furthered the interests of victims and the interest of justice in cases in which the respondent had observed them.

The Colorado survey also included some unique items. One such item was an open-ended question that asked about changes that respondents might want to victims' rights laws. Also, five items tested knowledge about Colorado state victims' rights laws. These items are as follows:

- who qualifies for victims' rights under Colorado law
- who decides whether victims provide input orally or in writing at sentencing
- of what kinds of events victims should be informed
- what the law says about awarding and payment of restitution
- what protections victims have under the law.

The items were multiple choice, with one correct answer and five incorrect choices per item. Copies of the Colorado and three-state surveys are included in Appendix A and Appendix B, respectively.

The Colorado Survey

With the cooperation of professional associations for Colorado judges, prosecutors, victim advocates, public defenders, and the private bar, invitations to participate in the survey were sent to membership lists via email. The invitations were followed up by two email reminders sent at approximately two-week intervals. The first mailing discussed the survey purpose and invited participants to complete the survey online. Included in the initial letter was the survey URL and a unique ID. Each participant was allowed to complete only one survey, but each was able to change responses at any time as long as the survey remained open. Neither research staff nor the professional associations were able to determine who had taken the survey, nor could they connect survey responses to particular individuals.

Baseline Survey Response Rates

In all, 1,918 invitations were issued for the baseline survey in Colorado, and 378 surveys were completed, a 20-percent success rate. However, the response rates varied substantially according to the type of professional group, and a poor showing by defense attorneys was responsible for pulling down the overall rate (see Table 3.1). For public defenders, the completion rate was 12 percent, and, for private defense attorneys, the rate was just 8 percent. On the other hand, victim advocates had a completion rate of 97 percent, and, for prosecutors, the rate was 69 percent. The response rate for judges was 29 percent. The low response rates for defense attorneys and judges raise concerns about whether the responses are representative of those populations. This is especially concerning because we do not have any information on nonresponders to use in order to determine where they are similar to those who did respond to the survey.

Opinions About Victims' Rights

Three-quarters of Colorado respondents agreed that victims ought to have explicit rights in the criminal justice process. Nearly half (49 percent) reported believing that victims should have legal standing in order to enforce their rights in court. A slightly smaller proportion (44 percent) said that there should be remedies for victims whose rights are denied. However, not even one in three (32 percent) said that victims should have the option of being represented by an attorney, and just one in five (21 percent) agreed that victims' rights attorneys could be helpful to the respondent. Moreover, fully two in three respondents (66 percent) said that victims' rights often conflict with the rights of the accused.

However, we found substantial differences in opinions about victims' rights according to profession. Not surprisingly, victim advocates expressed the most-positive attitudes and defense attorneys the least positive attitudes. Judges and prosecutors generally held similar attitudes that fell between the other two groups (see Figure 3.1).

Virtually all victim advocates (99 percent) said that victims ought to have explicit rights in the criminal justice system. The overwhelming majority of both prosecutors (89 percent) and judges (90 percent) reported similar attitudes. At the other extreme, just 31 percent of defense attorneys shared this view. Opinions were just as diverse on the other questions about the role of victims in the adjudication process. A large majority (83 percent) of victim advocates

Table 3.1
Baseline Colorado Survey Response Rates

Surveys	Prosecutors	Victim Advocates	Judges	Public Defenders	Private Defense Bar
Total sent	211	60	404	354	889
Completed	146	58	118	42	68
Rate (%)	69	97	29	12	8

Figure 3.1
Baseline Opinions of Victims' Rights, by Profession, for Colorado Respondents

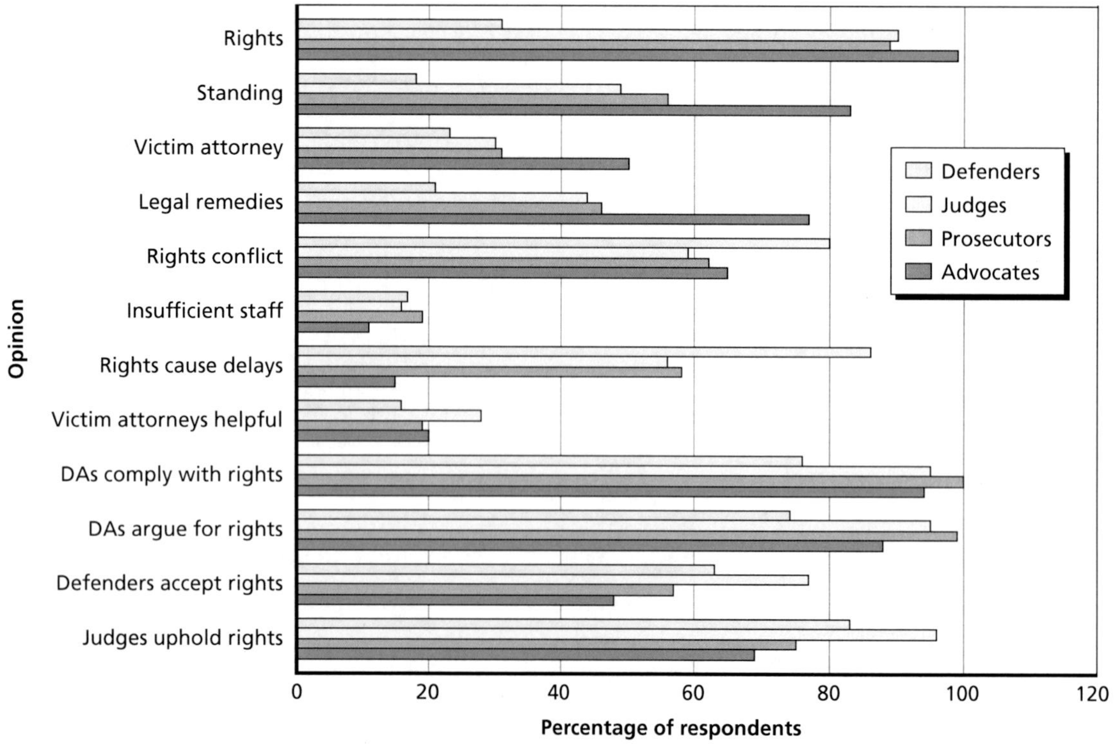

NOTE: Shows percentage of respondents who strongly agreed or agreed with the items listed earlier. DA = district attorney.
RAND TR1179-3.1

believed that victims ought to have legal standing in court, compared with about half of prosecutors (56 percent) and judges (49 percent), but just 18 percent of the defense attorneys. Three in four victim advocates (77 percent) stated that victims should be accorded legal remedies when rights were violated, while somewhat less than a majority of prosecutors (46 percent) and judges (44 percent) reported similar beliefs: Among defense attorneys, just 21 percent thought that victims ought to have legal remedies. The reluctance of defense attorneys to favor legal remedies for victims may stem from the fact that they overwhelmingly (80 percent) reported believing that victim and defendant rights often conflict. A majority of representatives from the other professions also felt that way, including 65 percent of victim advocates, 62 percent of prosecutors, and 59 percent of judges. Allowing victims to have attorneys was endorsed by half of victim advocates but by only a minority of respondents from the other professions (31 percent of prosecutors, 30 percent of judges, and 23 percent of defense attorneys).

The professions were also split on the practical implications of honoring victims' rights. A large majority (80–90 percent) of respondents in all the professions believed that their agencies were sufficiently staffed to comply with victims' rights legislation. However, although an overwhelming majority (86 percent) of defense attorneys stated that complying with victims' rights frequently delayed dispositions, this opinion was held by small majorities of prosecutors (58 percent) and judges (56 percent) and few victim advocates (15 percent).

All professions rated prosecutors' observance of victims' rights highly. Nine in ten or more victim advocates, judges, and prosecutors believed that prosecutors comply with victims' rights requirements and argue in court for victims' rights to be honored. Three in four defense attorneys held similar beliefs. Belief in judges' willingness to uphold victims' rights was very strong among judges (96 percent) but somewhat less strong among the other professions, with 75 percent of prosecutors, 69 percent of victim advocates, and 83 percent of defense attorneys sharing the belief that judges uphold victims' rights. A majority of representatives of most professions, including 77 percent of judges, 57 percent of prosecutors, and 63 percent of defense attorneys stated that defense attorneys accepted victims' rights. This sentiment was shared by a somewhat smaller proportion of victim advocates (48 percent).

Knowledge of Victims' Rights Laws

In addition to the opinion questions, the Colorado baseline survey included five questions to test respondents' factual knowledge of victims' rights. The questions tested knowledge of who qualifies for victims' rights under Colorado law, who decides whether victims provide input orally or in writing at sentencing, the kinds of events of which victims should be informed, what the law says about restitution, and what protections victims have under the law.

Respondents had the greatest knowledge of victims' rights related to protection: More than nine in ten correctly recognized which protections were afforded victims under Colorado law (see Figure 3.1). More than two in three respondents also correctly answered questions about the events of which victims had a right to be informed, who decides whether victims may provide written or oral input at sentencing (the correct answer is the victim), and who qualifies as a victim for purposes of victims' rights eligibility in Colorado. However, less than half of respondents correctly answered the question about restitution rights. When asked to identify the one true statement about restitution, respondents should have chosen that restitution is required in every case in which the victim suffers a pecuniary loss. Although the correct answer was the most frequently chosen, just 36 percent of those answering the question knew that restitution is mandatory in Colorado. One-quarter thought that the right to restitution appears in Colorado's victims' rights constitutional amendment (the provision is in the implementing legislation, not the constitution), 17 percent thought that restitution was available for pain and suffering (it is not), and 15 percent thought that restitution could not be ordered to be paid in one lump sum (it can).

The aggregate numbers mask large differences between different professions. In general, victim advocates more reliably had knowledge of victims' rights than members of the other professions, particularly judges and defense attorneys, had. Differences were especially pronounced on the question about who qualifies as a victim under Colorado law and who decides whether victims are able to make a written or oral statement and sentencing (see Table 3.2). But the pattern did not hold for all questions: On the question about restitution knowledge, a much lower percentage of victim advocates knew the correct response than the other three groups.

Ideas for Changes to Victims' Rights Laws

The Colorado survey contained a single open-ended item at the end: "What changes would you make to your state's victims' rights laws and/or the way that they are currently being implemented?" Answers to this question illuminated some of the specific concerns and ideas each professional group had about victims' rights.

Seventeen *victim advocates* made comments about victims' rights laws and their implementation. The most common theme that emerged in the victim advocates' responses was that

Table 3.2
Proportion of Correct Responses to Questions About Victims' Rights, by Profession, for Colorado Respondents (%)

Item	Victim Advocates (n = 72)	Prosecutors (n = 146)	Defense Attorneys (n = 125)	Judges (n = 122)	Total (N = 465)
Who qualifies for victims' rights under Colorado law	95	83	26	64	67
Who decides whether victims provide input orally or in writing at sentencing	82	79	61	62	71
The kinds of events of which victims should be informed	83	71	55	68	68
What the law says about awarding and payment of restitution	29	53	49	49	48
What protections victims have under the law	89	92	88	97	92

there needs to be more mandated training on victims' rights for criminal justice officials, particularly judges and prosecutors. Some felt that these professionals needed to have more victim sensitivity, as well as a better understanding of domestic violence and sexual assault dynamics.

Several comments specifically targeted judges, saying that, in addition to more training, there needed to be more accountability when judges violate victims' rights. One respondent commented that the requirement that a victim try to rectify the denial of his or her rights directly with the violating party before filing a complaint with the state is intimidating when the violating party is a judge.

Another complaint brought up by several victim advocates was the number of continuances that are regularly granted to defendants. Two advocates commented that victims are revictimized when cases are drawn out over long periods of time. They argued for a limit on the number of continuances granted.

Thirty-one *prosecutors* made comments on victims' rights and their implementation. A recurrent theme in the prosecutors' comments was that complying with victim notification often leads to a great deal of wasted time trying to track down victims who do not keep their contact information up to date or do not want to cooperate with the prosecution. Several felt that victims should have to opt in for notifications, and some suggested that, if contact is attempted and the victim does not respond, the prosecutor's duty to notify should be considered fulfilled. Several prosecutors felt that, because it is a state mandate, the victims' rights amendment (VRA) should be state funded to give prosecutors more resources to comply with its provisions. On the other hand, several prosecutors felt that the victims' rights laws worked well and that no changes were needed.

The most common theme among the 27 *judges* who responded was that victims' rights laws worked well and that continued training was needed for all parties. Nonetheless, two judges expressed concern about any expansion of victims' rights, with one saying that the criminal justice system is simply not built as a forum for victims and another stating that victims should not be allowed to "dictate" pleas or sentences because this could lead to wide disparities and create a due-process problem. On the other hand, a few judges felt that the law or its implementation does not go far enough. Two said that some serious crimes are not included in the VRA but should be.

Two judges had practical ideas for better ensuring compliance with victims' rights. One suggested that law enforcement be required to include with the paperwork documentation that the victim had been notified of his or her right to be present at first appearance of the defendant and that, given such notification, a victim should be required to either be present at that appearance (usually the bond hearing) or waive, in writing, his or her right to be there. The respondent said that this would help judges better gauge whether victims' rights had actually been complied with. Another judge suggested that VRA cases should be flagged by a different-color folder and should include a checklist to help judges ensure compliance with the rights.

Defense attorneys had the most to say. Nine felt that victims' rights should be abolished, but the vast majority of comments included some specific complaints about the way the system is currently working and some suggestions for improvement. The most commonly raised objection to victims' rights was that they interfere with defendants' constitutional rights. The Constitution was mentioned 18 times in the defense attorneys' comments. Several felt that victims' rights upset the balance and fairness of the courtroom, and four specifically alluded to the presumption of innocence guaranteed by the Constitution. Several also argued that the criminal justice process is "not about the victim" and that the civil arena is a better place for victims to air their concerns and have their needs met.

Another common complaint was that prosecutors use victims' rights only to further their own agendas and essentially ignore victims who want a "softer" approach than the prosecutor does or who want charges dropped. The next most common complaint was that proceedings were delayed by prosecutors who failed to notify victims. The defenders found this most problematic at bond hearings, when the failure to notify the victim meant that bond could not be posted and the defendant would have to remain incarcerated, sometimes risking job loss or other collateral consequences.

Colorado Post–Clinic Opening Survey Response Rates

The second survey wave for Colorado, approximately one year after the first wave, was not nearly as successful as the first, even though the methods used were identical. Table 3.3 depicts the number of completed surveys for each of the waves. In general, second-wave responses were a small fraction of completions for the first survey wave. No defense attorney surveys were obtained for the second wave because we were unable to regain the cooperation of professional associations for either the private bar or public defenders (who only reluctantly agreed to participate in the first survey wave). Despite the fact that survey invitations were again circulated by the state judicial and prosecutor organizations, fewer judges and prosecutors participated in the second survey.[1] The process for surveying victim advocates was also the same for the first and second phases, with the state organization for victim advocates supplying emails for the advocates, project staff issuing invitations directly to the advocates, and the state organization separately urging advocates to participate. However, their response rates were also substantially lower than those in the first phase. We suspect that the low response rates for the second wave of the survey resulted from failure of officials to understand the pre-post research design: It

---

[1]   To preserve anonymity of respondents, we did not track whether those who responded to the second wave of the survey also had responded to the first wave.

Table 3.3
Colorado Survey Completions, by
Profession, Waves 1 and 2 Compared

Profession	Wave 1	Wave 2	Total
Victim advocates	72	13	85
Prosecutors	146	20	166
Judges	122	30	152
Defense attorneys	125	0	125

may be that many officials did not see a reason to respond to a survey identical to one to which they had responded 12 months earlier.

Comparison of Responses from Two Colorado Survey Waves

In order to determine whether there was a change in opinions from the first to the second survey wave, we created a composite scale by averaging the eight items measuring opinions about victims' rights (provided on the first page of this chapter).[2] A reliability analysis showed that the eight items yielded an alpha coefficient of 0.71, a value that justified creating a scale based on the mean of all nonmissing values for the eight items.

The mean scores for survey waves 1 and 2 are presented in Table 3.4 broken down by profession. It is apparent that, for the three professional groups for which we have both pre- and postclinic data, the mean opinion scores for the second survey wave are higher than for the first wave, indicating a shift toward more-favorable attitudes toward victims' rights in wave 2. The overall difference between waves was statistically significant.[3]

In order to be sure that the wave 1–wave 2 difference was due to changes within professions and not to a different distribution of professions (e.g., more victim advocates who tend to have more-positive opinions about victims' rights in the wave 2 sample), we ran a second test that included terms for both survey wave and profession, as well as an interaction term. This analysis of variance showed a significant effect of both profession ($F[2,490] = 16.76$, $p < 0.001$)

Table 3.4
Colorado Attitudes Toward Victims'
Rights, Means, by Profession, Waves
1 and 2 Compared

Profession	Wave 1	Wave 2
Victim advocates	3.50	3.81
Prosecutors	3.18	3.42
Judges	3.23	3.53
Defense attorneys	2.76	N/A

NOTE: N/A = not applicable.

---

[2]   Scale items that were negatively worded were reverse-coded before taking the average of items.

[3] $F[3,493] = 20.93$, $p < 0.001$. F is a statistic based on analysis of variance used to determine whether a result is likely due to chance or to a real effect.

and wave (F[1,490] = 12.30, p < 0.001) but no significant interaction effect (F[2,490] = 0.24, not significant [n.s.]).

We conducted a similar analysis of differences between survey waves for the questions about compliance with victims' rights (the four items are given on the second page of this chapter) among prosecutors, judges, and defense attorneys. Again, we began by conducting a reliability analysis of the four items that assessed support for victims' rights among criminal justice officials. The reliability coefficient of 0.74 suggested that it was appropriate to create a composite scale based on averaging the four items. The scale was created by calculating a mean score from all nonmissing values for the four items.

Table 3.5 shows the composite victims' rights compliance scores for the two waves broken down by profession of the respondents. The most optimistic view of criminal justice official support for victims' rights was found among judges and prosecutors, while defense attorneys and victim advocates were the least optimistic. Among all the professional groups, there was an increase in optimism about official compliance for victims' rights from the first to the second survey wave. Analysis of variance confirmed a statistically significant effect of profession (F[2,479] = 11.14, p < 0.001) and survey wave (F[1,479] = 7.95, p < 0.005).[4]

The final table in this section, Table 3.6, shows the number of correct answers to the factual questions about victims' rights statutes, broken down by profession and survey wave. It shows that judges scored the most right answers, followed by prosecutors, victim advocates, and defense attorneys. There is no consistent difference across survey waves. Analysis of vari-

Table 3.5
Colorado Victims' Rights Support, Means, by Profession, Waves 1 and 2 Compared

Profession	Wave 1	Wave 2
Victim advocates	3.88	4.04
Prosecutors	4.13	4.35
Judges	4.17	4.55
Defense attorneys	3.76	N/A

Table 3.6
Colorado Victims' Rights Knowledge Test, Means, by Profession, Waves 1 and 2 Compared

Profession	Wave 1	Wave 2
Victim advocates	2.85	2.46
Prosecutors	3.23	3.20
Judges	2.45	2.63
Defense attorneys	1.86	N/A

---

[4] The interaction term was not statistically significant (F[2,279] = 0.63, n.s.).

ance confirmed a statistically significant effect of profession ($F_{[2,397]} = 4.86$, $p < 0.01$) and failed to confirm a significant effect of survey wave ($F_{[1,397]} = 0.14$, n.s.).[5]

The results indicate that there was a positive shift both in attitudes toward victims' rights and in compliance with victims' rights over the approximately one-year period between surveys, coincident with the establishment of the Colorado victims' rights clinic. Of course, this evidence is correlational in nature: We cannot establish with any certainty that the observed shift in attitudes was due to the establishment of the clinic, but it is *consistent* with the idea that establishing the clinics would change attitudes of criminal justice officials toward victims' rights. Moreover, it is concerning that the second survey wave sample is much smaller than the initial sample. It could be argued that the smaller number of respondents who completed the second survey were more sympathetic to victims' rights issues. If true, that could explain why attitudes on the second survey wave were more positive. But, if that hypothesis were true, we would expect that second-wave respondents would have been more knowledgeable about victims' rights issues, and, as can be observed in Table 3.6, that was not the case.

The Maryland, South Carolina, and Utah Surveys

In the three other states, we did not have the opportunity to conduct pre- and postclinic surveys with criminal justice officials. Instead, we asked survey respondents to assess their opinions about victims' rights and perceptions of compliance with victims' rights by court officials. We further asked them to make similar assessments about their opinions and attitudes six years ago—a time before the clinics in these states opened their doors. In addition, we asked survey respondents to tell us about their experience with their state's victims' rights clinic and whether the clinic had influenced them on victims' rights issues. We recognize that there are significant problems with this type of retrospective analysis, but, in this case, it was the only option available.

In Maryland, an invitation was forwarded via email by the Maryland State's Attorneys' Association to the 24 state's attorney's offices, with a follow-up email. Eight prosecutors participated. An invitation to 140 state victim advocates and follow-up email were forwarded through a state advocate email list, and 43 of them took part. An invitation was also forwarded to the Maryland Criminal Defense Attorneys Association, an organization of 450 members. A total of 11 defense attorneys completed the survey. Despite repeated contacts, the court system did not respond to requests for assistance in distributing the survey. Instead, 258 judges were sent invitations in the mail, with a follow-up letter two weeks later. A total of 34 judges participated in the survey.

In South Carolina, executive director of the South Carolina Commission on Prosecution Coordination suggested we approach the solicitors directly. We emailed the 16 circuit solicitors and urged to extend the invitation to prosecutors on their staff, sending a reminder two weeks later. Twelve participated. The South Carolina Commission on Indigent Defense administrator forwarded the survey invitation to the state's 16 public defenders, who were urged to distribute it to their staff. A total of 26 defense attorneys participated. After several contacts, we were unable to secure the assistance of the judges' association. Instead, survey invitations were mailed to 369 judges, with a follow-up mailing two weeks later. A total of 60 participated. The

---

[5] The interaction term was not statistically significant ($F_{[2,397]} = 0.62$, n.s.).

South Carolina Law Enforcement Victim Advocate Association forwarded our invitation; project staff also issued an invitation and follow-up through the association's email lists of South Carolina victim advocates, compiled through recent state-level trainings. A total of 60 advocates were invited to participate, and 43 did so.

In Utah, the Utah Prosecution Council distributed the invitation to its 515 members; 77 participated in the survey. The Utah Association of Criminal Defense Lawyers also distributed to its 350 members; 42 participated. The statewide victims' advocate organization distributed the invitation to its 164 members; 74 responded. The administrative office of the courts declined to forward the invitation, so project staff mailed invitations to 209 judges; 26 participated.

Completion rates are depicted in Table 3.7.

Respondents to the surveys in Maryland, South Carolina, and Utah were asked the same set of eight questions to elicit their opinions on victims' rights that the Colorado respondents were asked (provided on the first page of this chapter). Again, we created a scale taking the mean of the items. The resulting scale had a range of 1 (least favorable) to 5 (most favorable). The means are displayed in Table 3.8, broken down by states and professions of the respondents. Overall, South Carolina respondents had the most-positive opinions of victims' rights and Maryland the least, in part due to the very low favorable opinions among Maryland defense attorneys.

As we saw in Colorado, victim advocates across the three states had the most favorable view of victims' rights, prosecutors and judges were the next most favorable, and defense attorneys the least favorable. An analysis of variance for repeated measures confirmed a main effect

Table 3.7
Survey Completes for Three States

Respondent	Number of Invitations Issued	Number Complete	Completion Rate (%)
Maryland		96	
Victim advocates	140	43	31
Prosecutors	Unknown	8	—
Judges	258	34	13
Defense attorneys	450	11	2
South Carolina		141	
Victim advocates	60	43	72
Prosecutors	Unknown	12	—
Judges	369	60	16
Defense attorneys	Unknown	26	—
Utah		219	
Victim advocates	164	74	45
Prosecutors	515	77	15
Judges	209	26	12
Defense attorneys	350	42	12

Table 3.8
Changes in Opinions About Victims' Rights in Three States

Respondent	Now	6 Years Ago	Change (%)
Maryland	3.36	3.29	+0.02
Victim advocates	3.91	3.75	+0.04
Prosecutors	3.11	3.09	+0.01
Judges	3.09	3.04	+0.02
Defense attorneys	2.39	2.57	−0.07
South Carolina	3.60	3.54	+0.02
Victim advocates	3.98	3.83	+0.04
Prosecutors	2.65	2.84	−0.07
Judges	3.45	3.29	+0.05
Defense attorneys	3.30	3.58	−0.08
Utah	3.53	3.44	+0.03
Victim advocates	4.03	3.75	+0.07
Prosecutors	3.29	3.24	+0.02
Judges	3.74	3.59	+0.04
Defense attorneys	2.93	3.22	−0.09

of profession.[6] In general, respondents felt that their opinions of victims' rights had become more positive over time, but the overall change among officials was not statistically significant.[7] There was, however, a statistically significant interaction of profession and time: Although prosecutors, judges, and victim advocates reported that their opinions had become more positive over time, defense attorneys actually reported that their opinions toward victims' rights had become less favorable over the six-year interval.[8] This may reflect pushback among defense attorneys reacting to the expansion of victims' rights.

We also created a composite measure of compliance with victims' rights by averaging responses to individual items (the four items given on the second page of this chapter), as we had for the Colorado survey. Again, the scale ranged from 1 (least compliant) to 5 (most compliant). On this measure, differences between states were minimal. On the compliance measure, victim advocates were the least likely of the four professions to believe that court officials were in compliance on victims' rights statutory requirements (see Table 3.9). The other three professions were similar and quite positive in their beliefs that court officials complied with victims' rights requirements. An analysis of repeated measures test confirmed a statistically significant difference between professions.[9] But the most striking thing in Table 3.9 is the large

[6] $F[3,375] = 44.44$, $p < 0.001$.

[7] $F[1,375] = 0.065$, n.s.

[8] $F[3,371] = 18.47$, $p < 0.001$.

[9] $F[3,322] = 16.17$, $p < 0.001$.

Table 3.9
Changes in Perceptions of Court Official Compliance with Victims' Rights Laws in Three States

Respondent	Now	6 Years Ago	Change (%)
Maryland	3.83	3.52	+0.09
Victim advocates	3.48	3.15	+0.10
Prosecutors	4.06	4.00	+0.02
Judges	4.13	3.84	+0.08
Defense attorneys	4.04	3.49	+0.16
South Carolina	3.89	3.48	+0.12
Victim advocates	3.39	2.87	+0.19
Prosecutors	4.17	3.89	+0.07
Judges	4.03	3.64	+0.11
Defense attorneys	4.02	3.60	+0.12
Utah	3.78	3.45	+0.10
Victim advocates	3.65	3.16	+0.16
Prosecutors	3.79	3.53	+0.07
Judges	4.06	3.83	+0.06
Defense attorneys	3.88	3.66	+0.06

positive shift in perceptions of compliance for all professions in all three states.[10] Percentage increases in mean compliance scale ratings ranged from 0.02 to 0.19, with the largest increases clustered among victim advocates.

Officials in Maryland, South Carolina, and Utah were also asked about their experiences with victims' rights clinic staff. Overall, 49 percent of court officials reported at least one contact with clinic attorneys. Prosecutors and victim advocates were more likely than judges and defense attorneys to report contact. Although the numbers of cases in several cells are quite small, it is worth noting that there is a striking difference between states in Table 3.10: Prosecutors and victim advocates in South Carolina were less than half as likely to report contact with a clinic attorney as their counterparts in Utah and Maryland.

Officials who had had contact with a clinic attorney were asked to evaluate the attorney's performance. Because those who reported contact were a subset of the entire sample, numbers were too small to break responses down by both state and profession. Table 3.11 reports results by profession only. Victim advocates had the most-favorable views of the work of clinic attorneys. A large majority believed that the clinic's intervention had furthered both the interest of the victim and the interest of justice. Among prosecutors and judges, about half believed that the victims' rights attorney had the effect of furthering the interests of the victim and of justice. Only one-quarter of defense attorneys believed that the clinic attorney had furthered

---

[10] $F[1,322] = 14.53$, $p < 0.001$.

Table 3.10
Contact with Clinic Staff in Three States
(percentage who answered positively)

Respondent	Had Contact with Clinic	
	%	n
Maryland		
Victim advocates	71	21
Prosecutors	50	6
Judges	32	7
Defense attorneys	29	22
South Carolina		
Victim advocates	20	25
Prosecutors	25	8
Judges	33	18
Defense attorneys	22	49
Utah		
Victim advocates	87	60
Prosecutors	64	66
Judges	29	35
Defense attorneys	37	21

Table 3.11
Evaluation of Clinic Work in Three States (percentage who had contact with a clinic attorney)

Respondent	Clinic's Intervention Furthered Interest of Victim	Clinic's Intervention Furthered Interest of Justice	Contact with Clinic Positively Changed View of Victim Rights
Victim advocates	76	80	61
Prosecutors	52	43	30
Judges	45	56	39
Defense attorneys	28	12	9
Overall	57	58	44

the interests of the victim, and only 12 percent believed that the attorney's involvement had furthered the interest of justice.

According to survey respondents, contact with victims' rights attorneys had a significant impact on their views of victims' rights. Fully 61 percent of victim advocates, 30 percent of prosecutors, and 39 percent of judges said that the experience with a clinic attorney had made them feel more favorable toward victims' rights. Among defense attorneys, however, only 9 percent reported being influenced to adopt a more favorable view of victims' rights (and, in fact, 35 percent of defense attorneys reported that their contact with a clinic attorney had made them feel *less* favorably about victims' rights).

Summary

In Colorado, where we had both pre- and postclinic data on opinions about victims' rights, we found a shift toward more-favorable attitudes toward victims' rights following the opening of the victims' rights clinic. Similarly, we found in Colorado a shift toward greater perceived compliance with victims' rights statutes after the clinic opened. Knowledge of specific victims' rights contained in Colorado statutes did not increase preclinic to postclinic.

In the three states where we had to rely on respondents' retrospective reports, respondents reported shifts toward more-positive attitudes toward victims' rights in each of the three states following the opening of the victims' rights clinics. The change was small but consistent within each professional group: prosecutors, victim advocates, and judges. In contrast, defense attorneys in each state believed that their opinions about victims' rights had become more negative over time. We observed larger shifts when asking about compliance with victims' rights. Each group of professionals—including defense attorneys—in all three states believed that compliance with victims' rights legislation had improved since the clinics had been founded. Of course, we cannot know for certain whether the shift in perceptions was caused wholly or in part by the clinics. But the observed changes are consistent with the stated purpose of the clinics.

CHAPTER FOUR

Determining Compliance with Victims' Rights, Based on Prosecutor Records

One of the ways to assess the impact that clinics have had on the extent to which victims' rights are honored is through analysis of court records. By comparing compliance with rights in individual cases before the clinic opened and cases in which the clinic represented the victims, we can gain a better understanding of how clinics directly affect the behavior of court officials in individual cases through advocacy work. By further comparing cases in which victims are represented by clinic attorneys and current cases in which victims have no representation, we can gain an understanding of the indirect effect of the clinic's presence through changes that the clinic has brought about to case law and court rules and changes in the attitudes of court officials toward victims' rights.

Evaluation Plan

Evaluability assessments conducted during our process evaluation revealed that there does not exist in any of the clinic sites a statewide database that reliably and comprehensively records information on observance of victims' rights. We determined that the best sources of information were prosecutor files. This is true because it is largely prosecutors who are responsible for ensuring compliance with victims' rights. The evaluability assessment found that most of the information we sought is recorded by the prosecutor's office in the principal jurisdiction in which each of the eight clinics work.

We recognized that there would be problems with using prosecutor files for this purpose: First, information on compliance with victims' rights generally is not entered into a computer database, so we would need to sample and abstract information from paper files. Second, few offices have checkboxes for victims' rights compliance; rather, compliance information generally has to be searched for in the files. Third, we expected to encounter significant amounts of missing data. However, we did similar work using prosecutor case files in six locations in North Carolina and Wisconsin for a study on victims' rights several years ago (Davis, Henderson, and Rabbitt, 2002), and the data collection, although time-consuming, worked quite well.

To determine the effect that clinics have had on observance of victims' rights, we planned to collect three samples of cases from prosecutor files in the jurisdiction or jurisdictions in which each local clinic has done the most work: (1) all clinic cases closed since the start of each local clinic, (2) cases closed during the most recent 12-month period that did not involve representation by a clinic attorney, and (3) cases closed in the year prior to the start of each local clinic.

We realized that the sampling process would, of necessity, be idiosyncratic to each jurisdiction because of differences in ways that files are cataloged and availability of computer search capabilities to aid in the sampling process. Still, we tried to proceed following common rules. We began by asking clinic staff to identify all closed cases in which clinics had signed representation agreements in the targeted jurisdictions.

Once the clinic sample was drawn in each state, we drew the baseline samples from prosecutor files in a manner that would ensure that it would be as similar as possible to the clinic sample in terms of county of origin and type of crime. For example, because 62 percent of the Prince George's, Maryland, sample of clinic cases consisted of homicides, we tried to match that distribution in the baseline prosecutor sample for that state. (In fact, the completed preclinic sample contained 66 percent homicides, and the postclinic nonattorney cases contained 64 percent homicides.)

The number of baseline cases sampled was keyed to the number of clinic cases in that state. Because we expected to have a lower success rate with victim interviews in the prosecutor samples than in the clinic samples, we oversampled prosecutor files by 50 percent. We developed a tailored sampling methodology for each participating prosecutor's office based on each office's filing system and computer capabilities. Where possible, we sampled cases within each crime category randomly from computer databases. For situations in which a site lacked the capability to sample from computer files, we developed a scheme for obtaining a representative sample from manual files.

The process for drawing the concurrent sample of nonclinic cases from prosecutor files was the same as that used for the archival sample. The only difference was that, in the concurrent sample of nonclinic cases, we needed to check each sampled case to make sure that it was not a clinic case. As with the baseline sample, we oversampled the concurrent nonclinic cases by 50 percent.

Table 4.1 summarizes sampling methods from each of the seven sites included in the study.

Our targeted sample sizes were 300 total clinic cases and 450 pre- and postclinic comparison cases. The final sample of 757 cases included 174 clinic cases, 282 preclinic cases, and 297 postclinic cases not represented by a victims' rights attorney. As we had planned, most of the cases were from Utah (n = 525), followed by Maryland (n = 170) and South Carolina (n = 61) (see Figure 4.1). Sample sizes were smaller than expected for the clinic samples and, therefore, for the baseline and postclinic prosecutor samples (because the sizes of the later two samples were calculated at 150 percent of the clinic samples). The primary reasons for smaller-than-expected clinic samples were cases that had not been filed with the court in the targeted jurisdictions (mainly cases in which the attorney helped with getting a restraining order) and cases in which the clinic files did not contain a court docket number so that we could not look up the case in the prosecutors' files.

Across the seven sites, the most-frequent types of cases involved assault or attempted murder (n = 216), followed by homicide (n = 133), child sex abuse (n = 112), domestic violence or stalking (n = 102), sexual assault (n = 91), robbery or kidnapping (n = 36), theft or white-collar crime (n = 17), and other (n = 43) (see Figure 4.2).[1]

---

[1] *Other* includes disturbing the peace, disorderly conduct, interfering with a police officer, reckless conduct, trespass, harassment, and violation of pretrial release.

Table 4.1
Sampling Methods for Each Study Site

Site	Method
Md., Prince George's County	Baseline and postclinic cases were sampled from printouts organized by case type (e.g., homicides, sexual assaults). For each case type list, we counted up the number of cases and divided by the number of that type of case needed, then sampled every nth case on the list. (Example: If there were 100 homicides and we needed 20, we divided 100 by 20 and then sampled every fifth case.) For preclinic cases, we gathered information from computer records and case files. For postclinic cases, no paper files were available, so we relied exclusively on computer records.
Md., Baltimore City	Sampling by computer lists was impossible, and we were not allowed in the file room. Therefore, we had to rely on state's attorney staff to draw the baseline and postclinic samples for us. We instructed them on the number of each type of case that we sought and on methods to draw systematic samples within each case type. Because most baseline case files had been destroyed, we were unable to achieve our target numbers for that sample. Information was derived both from case files and from a computer database of victims who had returned initial notification forms.
S.C., District 9	We were able to sample from computer lists broken down by type of crime. Sampling proceeded in the same way as described above for Prince George's County cases. Information was drawn from victim advocate files.
S.C., District 4	We were not able to sample by computer or logs, so we had to sample from the files themselves. Because files were not organized by type of crime, it was difficult to sample systematically. What we were able to do was to try to ensure that, within each crime type, cases were spread relatively evenly throughout the year. No information was available on computer, so we drew information only from the paper files. No victim contact information was available, so we were unable to attempt any interviews for District 4.
Utah, Cache County	We sampled from a victim advocate computer database using a methodology similar to that described above for Prince George's County, Md., and South Carolina's District 9. Information was gathered from both computerized and paper victim advocate files.
Utah, Salt Lake City	We sampled from a prosecutor's computer database using a methodology similar to that described above for Prince George's County, Md., and South Carolina's District 9. The city office prosecutes only misdemeanors; more-serious offenses are prosecuted by Salt Lake County. We relied on the computerized prosecutor files. To construct the sample, we instructed the prosecutor to take every fifth case of the particular case type over the specified time periods. We recorded information that was available from the docket sheets. Other victim information was available only on the prosecutor's proprietary computer system. For those fields, the prosecutor recorded the data in a Microsoft Excel spreadsheet.
Utah, Salt Lake County	We sampled from a prosecutor's computer database using a methodology similar to that described above for Prince George's County, Md., and South Carolina's District 9. After being provided with a list of the relevant cases from the specified time periods, we created a random sample by selecting every fourth or fifth case as necessary. As in Salt Lake City, we collected the relevant information that was publicly available from the docket sheets. Other information was available only in PIMS. To avoid attorney–client privilege issues, we hired a paralegal working in the office to abstract additional data that we needed.

NOTE: PIMS = Prosecutor Information Management System.

Data Abstraction

For all cases drawn into each of the three samples, we aimed to record the charge, case disposition, number of phone or in-person contacts between prosecutor staff and victims, and the following information about observance of victims' rights:

- whether the victim was given notice of his or her rights when a case was filed in court
- whether the victim was notified when the defendant was released from custody

Figure 4.1
Case File Sample Sizes, by Site

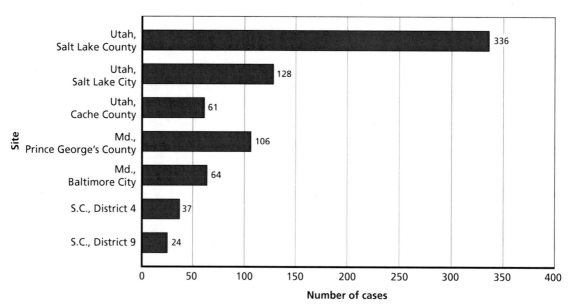

RAND *TR1179-4.1*

Figure 4.2
Types of Crimes in the Case File Sample

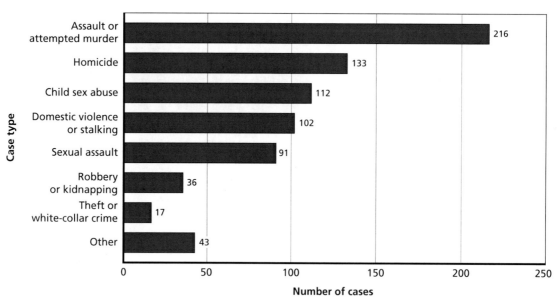

RAND *TR1179-4.2*

- whether the victim was consulted on plea offers
- whether the victim was offered the chance to make a victim-impact statement and whether he or she did make an oral statement to the court or file a written statement
- whether the victim was notified of the sentence
- whether the victim was asked about crime-related losses

- whether restitution was ordered.

Information on whether victims were sent an initial notification package and whether a victim-impact statement (VIS) was submitted was available for all sites. Information on whether restitution was ordered was available for both Maryland sites and for the two Salt Lake jurisdictions; data on whether information on victim financial losses was submitted to the court were available for the two South Carolina sites and Cache County. Finally, we were able to gather information on whether victims were consulted on plea agreements or had signed up for the Victim Information and Notification Everyday (VINE) in Baltimore City and Salt Lake County.[2] In all sites, we noted whether there was information in the file indicating that each of the various rights was observed. We believe that, in many instances in which rights were observed, the information either was not recorded or was lost over time. Thus, the estimates we developed are likely very conservative, but we hope that the errors were distributed in a relatively even manner over the clinic, baseline, and postclinic comparison samples.

Data Analysis Plan

In order to determine whether the victims' rights clinics had an effect on the observance of victims' rights, we compared clinic cases with preclinic cases and postclinic cases in which victims were not represented by attorneys. We expected that rights would be observed most often in cases in which victims were represented by attorneys. We also thought that we might detect greater observance of victims' rights in the postclinic nonattorney cases than in preclinic cases: This could be true if the example set by clinic attorneys "spilled over" or diffused to other cases.

After cleaning the data and checking for integrity, we combined data from the seven sites into a single database that included a variable for site identification. Dependent measures used in the analyses included each of the above-listed dichotomous compliance items. With total Ns of 174 clinic cases and 280 or more in each of the two comparison groups, the analyses had statistical power equal to 0.80 to detect as statistically significant proportional differences of at least 10 percentage points, assuming that we use a one-tailed test and an alpha criterion of 0.05. Smaller differences would probably not justify the public expenditures on the clinics.

After checking for comparability between samples in the type of crime (the only matching variables that we had available), we proceeded to run nonparametric tests of significance between the three samples for key variables, including observance of victims' rights and case disposition.

Findings

Table 4.2 presents a breakdown of various victims' rights by the three groups: clinic cases, preclinic cases, and postclinic cases not represented by a victims' rights attorney. As mentioned earlier, the Ns for each outcome variable differ because all sites did not have information on each of the rights. Differences between the three samples were generally small, and none

---

[2] VINE allows crime victims to obtain timely and reliable information about criminal cases and the custody status of offenders 24 hours a day.

Table 4.2
Compliance with Victims' Rights, by Sample (%)

Compliance	Clinic Cases	Preclinic Sample	Postclinic Sample
Victims informed of rights (N = 753)	76	70	70
Victims who submitted VIS (N = 753)	31	23	27
Victims submitting financial information to court (N = 631)	39	37	46
Victims informed of plea agreement (N = 397)	61	60	73
Victims subscribed to VINE notification (N = 397)	80	82	85
Victims receiving restitution orders (N = 122)	22	21	15

approached statistical significance in the proportions of victims (1) who received an initial notification of rights, (2) who submitted a VIS, (3) who submitted financial information on victim losses, (4) who were consulted about a plea agreement, (5) who had subscribed to VINE notification, and (6) who received restitution.

Because we had more-detailed information on victims' rights in Salt Lake County than in any of the other sites, we were able to conduct additional comparisons between the groups using that data set. For each of the variables representing notifying victims about their right to a court hearing, right to apply for compensation, right to restitution, right to privacy, right to protection, right to a speedy trial, and right to submit a VIS, the proportion of victims notified among clinic cases was 10–15 percentage points less than victims in either of the comparison groups. The unexpected direction of the difference between clinic cases and nonclinic cases might reflect underlying problems that caused the victims to retain the clinic.

Similarly, we did not observe any differences in favor of clinic victims in terms of the proportion of victims given information about victim services or the proportion of victims given referrals to victim services (see Table 4.3).

We did see some differences between the samples in individual sites in favor of clinic cases. In Prince George's County, victims represented by clinic attorneys were more likely to

Table 4.3
Observance of Victims' Rights, by Sample (Salt Lake County cases only) (%)

Observance	Clinic Cases	Preclinic Sample	Postclinic Sample
Victims informed of right to court hearing*** (N = 336)	81	92	94
Victims informed of right to compensation** (N = 336)	80	92	90
Victims informed of right to restitution** (N = 336)	80	92	90
Victims informed of right to privacy** (N = 336)	80	92	90
Victims informed of right to protection** (N = 336)	80	92	89
Victims informed of right to speedy trial** (N = 336)	80	92	89
Victims informed of right to submit VIS (N = 336)	42	57	58
Victims given information about victim services (N = 336)	68	56	76
Victims given referral to victim services*** (N = 336)	68	56	76

NOTE: ** = $p < 0.05$. *** = $p < 0.01$.

receive initial notification of rights than victims in the two comparison samples (81 percent of victims in clinic cases were informed, compared with 46 percent of preclinic controls and 56 percent of postclinic controls: Chi-square [2] = 7.88, p < 0.02).[3] In Baltimore City, victims in clinic cases were more likely to submit a VIS than victims in the two comparison groups (20 percent of victims represented by clinic attorneys submitted a VIS, compared with 0 percent of victims in the preclinic sample and 4 percent of victims in the postclinic sample: Chi-square [2] = 6.14, p < 0.05). In Salt Lake City, victims represented by clinic attorneys were more likely both to be informed of rights (53 percent of victims in clinic cases were informed, compared with 11 percent of victims in the preclinic comparison group and 6 percent of victims in the postclinic comparison group: Chi-square [2] = 30.57, p < 0.001) and to submit a VIS (28 percent of victims in clinic cases were informed, compared with 0 percent of victims in the preclinic comparison group and 0 percent of victims in the postclinic comparison group: Chi-square [2] = 27.72, p < 0.001). This number of significant differences is more than would be expected by chance in conducting 14 individual tests, if we assume the null hypothesis of no difference between clinic cases and controls. Still, the fact that there were no differences even approaching statistical significance over the three sites combined gives reason for skepticism about a true effect of the clinics on compliance with victims' rights based on criminal justice records.

We examined whether there were differences between clinic cases and the two comparison groups in the distribution of dispositions because of the hypothesis that representation by a clinic attorney might produce an increase in guilty pleas and a decrease in dismissals. Cases in which victims were represented by a victims' rights attorney were significantly less likely to be dismissed than cases in either comparison group: Seventeen percent of cases in the clinic group were dismissed, compared with 24 percent of preclinic cases and 29 percent of the postclinic comparison group (see Table 4.4). Conversely, clinic cases were more likely to result in a plea or plea in abeyance than cases in either of the other two groups:[4] Seventy-four percent of cases in

Table 4.4
Court Disposition, by Group (%)

Disposition	Clinic Cases (n = 142)	Preclinic Comparison Cases (n = 274)	Postclinic Comparison Cases (n = 280)
Dismissed	17	24	29
Plea in abeyance	12	8	4
Plea/no contest	62	58	55
Trial: convicted	6	6	10
Trial: not guilty	4	4	1
Abated by death	0	0	1
Total	100	100	100

NOTE: Totals may not sum to 100 because of rounding.

---

[3] The bracketed number (here, a 2) indicates the number of degrees of freedom.

[4] If a defendant receives a plea in abeyance, the case is put on hold while the defendant complies with the terms ordered by the judge. If the defendant successfully does so, the case is dismissed; if not, he or she is sentenced.

which victims were represented by clinic attorneys resulted in pleas, compared with 64 percent of the preclinic comparison group and 59 percent of the postclinic comparison group (Chi-square [10] = 26.71, p < 0.01). The proportion of trials was similar in each of the groups.

Finally, we examined whether the distribution of sentences was different between the three samples of cases. Those data, presented in Table 4.5, suggest that there were differences between the samples. It is obvious from the table that probation or fine and jail sentences are far more common in the clinic and preclinic comparison samples than in the postclinic comparison sample. Sixty-eight percent of clinic cases and 65 percent of preclinic comparison cases avoided prison terms one year or longer, compared with only 48 percent of the postclinic comparison group (Chi-square [2] = 15.10, p < 0.001). We do not have an explanation for the pattern of results, but they do not support an effect of the clinics on sentencing (nor was one expected).

Summary

We found that, in the seven prosecutors' offices with which we worked on this study, information about observance of victims' rights is at best spotty and at worst virtually nonexistent. Few offices had well-organized files on victims' rights, and, in those that did, the information was often lost after cases were disposed. This is not the situation that we expected to find but one that we were forced to adjust our data-collection plans to accommodate.

Across jurisdictions, we found no overall effect of having a victims' rights attorney on whether rights were honored reflected in the case files. This was true when we compared cases with victims' rights attorneys and an archival sample of similar cases, as well as when we compared cases with victims' rights attorneys and concurrent cases in which victims were not represented. We did find significant differences in three sites on the observance of some rights when victims were represented by clinic attorneys. We also found, across sites, that cases in

Table 4.5
Sentences, by Group (%)

Sentence	Clinic Cases (n = 109)	Preclinic Comparison Cases (n = 189)	Postclinic Comparison Cases (n = 186)
Probation or fine	37	36	23
Less than 1 year jail or time served	31	29	25
1–2 years in prison	5	7	8
3–5 years in prison	15	11	17
6–10 years in prison	2	8	11
11–20 years in prison	5	5	10
More than 20 years in prison	6	4	8
Juvenile detention	1	0	0
Total	100	100	100

NOTE: Totals may not sum to 100 because of rounding.

which victims had attorneys were less likely to be dismissed and more likely to result in guilty pleas than in cases without victims' rights attorneys, be they archival or concurrent cases.

CHAPTER FIVE

Surveys of Victim Experience in the Criminal Justice System

The principal goal of the crime-victim legal clinics is to assist individual victims by advocating for their rights and by assessing their social service needs and referring them to clinicians and other service programs. We also sought to assess the clinics' impact on victims' satisfaction with the criminal justice process and its compliance with their rights. To make these determinations, we conducted telephone interviews of two samples of victims in each evaluation site, one drawn from the sample of cases at prosecutor offices and crime-victim legal clinics.

To preserve victims' confidentiality, the initial contact with victims from cases in the prosecutor case-file samples was made by staff of the victims' rights clinics (for clinic cases) or prosecutors' staff (for nonclinic cases). Names and contact information for victims who agreed to participate were passed to NCVC staff to conduct interviews by phone.

The results of the victim contacts are presented in Table 5.1.

As the table shows, for only 27 percent of the files selected was the prosecutor's office or clinic able to identify and reach a victim. Some of the files selected did not have victim contact information. For many, the number listed was no longer working. And for others, the screener was never able to reach anyone after at five or more attempts, or the victim's phone blocked the call. Most of those contacted—90 percent—agreed to participate.

We were surprised that we were able to reach only 68 percent of the victims who had been prescreened based on their willingness to be interviewed. We surmise that most of the victims for whom we were unsuccessful after they had agreed to be interviewed screened their calls and chose not to answer a call from an unfamiliar number. During the last two weeks of the project period, after surveying staff reported that they were unable to reach a large number of victims, the outreach plan was adjusted to allow staff to leave a voice-mail message for the victim, leaving a call-back number and indicating they would also be called again. RAND and NCVC staff discussed the matter and determined that, because the victims had previously agreed to participate and because the telephone message indicated that the phone belonged to the victim, victim safety and right to sensitive treatment would not be compromised by leaving a message. As an additional precaution, the message left with the victim did not identify him or her as a victim of crime. Instead, it indicated that we had been given the victim's contact information as someone who would be willing to take a survey about legal rights, that the surveyor would try to reach them at another time, that they were also welcome to contact the surveyor directly, and that they would receive a payment for their time. The additional outreach effort also increased the amount of the participant payment, from $25 to $50. This additional outreach did prove productive and increased the numbers of eventual participants. As an illustration, staff was able to make contact with only 11 victims in the two weeks before altering the recruitment, compared with 25 victims in the two weeks after making the change.

Table 5.1
Results of Contact Attempts for Victim Survey

Contact	Case Files	With Victim Contact Data	Nonworking Number	No Answer or Blocked	Victim Refused Consent for Researcher Contact	Victim Consent Given for Researcher Contact	Researcher Unable to Contact Victim	Interviewed
S.C., Charleston prosecutor	18	16	9	1	0	6	3	3
S.C., clinic	80	80	32	2	1	45	15	30
Md., Baltimore state's attorney	46	10	1	6	1	2	0	2
Md., clinic	41	30	5	15	5	5	0	5
Utah, Cache County prosecutor	46	46	20	8	0	18	3 (and 1 refused to participate)	14
Utah, Salt Lake County prosecutor	267	257	196	29	4	28	7	21
Utah, Salt Lake City prosecutor	91	83	47	11	6	19	6	13
Utah, Cache County clinic	16	16	7	6	0	3	1	2
Utah, Salt Lake County clinic	71	71	22	3	2	44	21	23
Utah, Salt Lake City clinic	22	22	11	3	0	8	0	8

Table 5.2 compares the proportion of victims who said that specific rights were honored in cases with clinic attorneys and cases without clinic attorneys. We observed differences in favor of clinic cases in five of 11 categories of rights. Victims who had clinic attorneys were significantly more likely to receive notification of the defendant's pretrial release (58 percent versus 21 percent), more likely to have had someone protect the privacy of their medical records (56 percent versus 0 percent), more likely to make a VIS (94 percent versus 67 percent), more likely to receive help preparing a VIS (40 percent versus 8 percent), and more likely to be notified of the case disposition (92 percent versus 73 percent). There were no significant differences between victims with and without attorneys in the proportion who received initial notice of their rights, who were consulted by the prosecutor about a plea bargain, who were notified of the sentencing date, who were provided with an opportunity to make a VIS, who were asked about financial losses, or who received restitution.

Surprisingly, victims who had attorneys were less satisfied with the outcomes of their cases than victims without attorneys (see Figure 5.1). Among victims with attorneys, 41 per-

Surveys of Victim Experience in the Criminal Justice System   41

Table 5.2
Proportion of Victims Who Stated That Their Rights Were Honored, by Whether the Victim Had a Clinic Attorney (%)

Question	Clinic Case (n = 72)	Nonclinic Case (n = 53)
At any point after the crime was committed, were you given written or [spoken] notice of your rights as a crime victim?	56	65
Were you notified of the defendant's release?	58**	21**
Did anyone attempt to protect the privacy of medical records for you?	56**	0*
Did the prosecutor consult with you before making the plea offer?	59	50
Were you notified of the sentencing date?	63	57
Were you provided with the opportunity to make a victim-impact statement at sentencing?	69	60
Did you make a victim-impact statement?	94**	67
Did anyone help you prepare your statements?	40*	8*
Were you notified of the conviction or guilty plea?	92*	73*
Were you asked about crime-related losses for purposes of restitution?	61	53
Did the judge order restitution in your case?	24	32

NOTE: * = $p < 0.05$. ** = $p < 0.01$.

Figure 5.1
Satisfaction with Case Outcomes Among Victims With and Without Attorneys

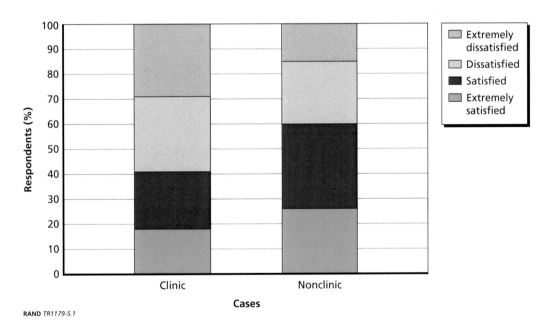

RAND *TR1179-5.1*

cent were extremely satisfied or satisfied with their case outcomes, compared with 60 percent of victims without attorneys.[1]

---

[1] Kendall's Tau C = −0.215, p < 0.03 based on ordinal scale: extremely satisfied, satisfied, dissatisfied, extremely dissatisfied.

This result is especially surprising in light of the data presented in Chapter Four that indicated that the attorney sample had fewer dismissals than the sample of cases in which victims did not have representation. There are several possible explanations for this surprising finding. It may be that those victims who turned to the clinics for assistance were those already experiencing problems in exercising their rights—or, in other words, clinic attorneys were dealing with the more-difficult cases. A similar explanation is that victims who are the most vocal and likely to complain are most likely to seek out attorneys and most likely to find fault with the actions of the justice system. Finally, it may be that victims' rights attorneys made clients more aware of their rights and what might result from prosecuting the case, but then victims were disappointed by what actually happened in court.

Victims were asked in the survey about their treatment by court officials, including prosecutors, judges, victim advocates, and defense attorneys. Overall, victims were most satisfied with their treatment by prosecutor victim advocates and least satisfied with their treatment by defense attorneys. Consistent with the finding on satisfaction with case outcomes, Table 5.3 shows that victims who were represented by clinic attorneys were significantly less satisfied with their treatment by victim advocates, prosecutors, and defense attorneys than victims who were not represented. Once again, this surprised us because we had expected that victims represented by clinic attorneys would have been treated better by court officials. Again, this may reflect raised awareness among victims who had attorneys or the possibility that the victims who sought attorneys were having problems having their rights respected.

Victims who had attorneys thought highly of them: Eighty percent reported being very satisfied with the way that their attorneys treated them. One male victim of workplace robbery felt that no one in the criminal justice system understood the severity of the crime or his significant ongoing safety concerns. However, he felt that the clinic attorney was 100 percent behind him, responding to all his calls, explaining every step in the process, and assuring him that he would support him. "That's what pulled me through, really." Another victim, the father of two sexual abuse victims, said, "I can't tell you how helpful [the clinic attorneys] were. . . . The system probably thinks it's victim friendly, but [it is] not." Another, the mother of a child victim, reported that "We wouldn't have gotten anywhere without the clinic."

We offered three items about victim satisfaction with the justice process: "I felt I had the power to exercise my rights as a crime victim during the criminal justice process," "My rights as a crime victim were respected," and "The criminal justice process was fair." Each of the three items offered five ordered response options: "Strongly agree" (1), "Agree" (2), "Neutral" (3), "Disagree" (4), and "Strongly disagree" (5). We created a scale based on the mean of these three items that proved to have good reliability (alpha = 0.89).

Figure 5.2 depicts means on the created scale. Means were significantly higher for clinic cases (mean [M] = 3.09, standard deviation [SD] = 1.36) than for nonclinic participants (M = 2.43, SD = 1.10).[2]

The means suggest that, although both groups were in the midrange of responses (neither positive nor negative), victims represented by attorneys were significantly less satisfied with the process than victims without attorneys.

Finally, we sought to determine whether victims who had attorneys were more often referred to services than other victims. Table 5.4 indicates clinic and nonclinic participants'

[2] $t_{(119)}$ = 2.912, p < 0.005.

Table 5.3
Treatment by Court Officials (%)

Treatment	Clinic Cases	Nonclinic Cases
Treatment by prosecutor**	(n = 66)	(n = 52)
Extremely satisfied	29	54
Satisfied	26	27
Dissatisfied	20	12
Extremely dissatisfied	26	8
Treatment by judge	(n = 60)	(n = 39)
Extremely satisfied	30	39
Satisfied	38	41
Dissatisfied	15	10
Extremely dissatisfied	17	10
Treatment by victim advocate**	(n = 52)	(n = 43)
Extremely satisfied	44	81
Satisfied	35	16
Dissatisfied	15	2
Extremely dissatisfied	6	0
Treatment by defense attorney**	(n = 47)	(n = 32)
Extremely satisfied	9	13
Satisfied	30	59
Dissatisfied	23	13
Extremely dissatisfied	38	16
Treatment by clinic attorney	(n = 62)	—
Extremely satisfied	80	—
Satisfied	13	—
Dissatisfied	7	—
Extremely dissatisfied	2	—

NOTE: * = $p < 0.05$. ** = $p < 0.01$ by Kendall's Tau C. Totals may not sum to 100 because of rounding.

referral to various services. Referrals were made with some frequency (greater than one in five victims) only for counseling, financial assistance, and protective orders. The remaining types of referrals (safe housing, medical provider, support group, transportation, and crime-scene cleanup) were few in number, presumably because these are needs that are relevant to only small numbers of victims. One significant difference was found between cases in which the victim was represented by a clinic attorney and nonattorney cases: Forty percent of victims

Figure 5.2
Satisfaction with Criminal Justice Process Among Victims With and Without Attorneys

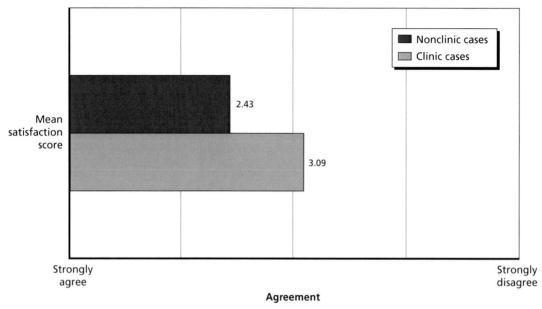

Table 5.4
Proportion of Victims Who Received Social Service Referrals, by Whether the Victim Had a Clinic Attorney (%)

Question: Did anyone refer you to a	Clinic Case (n = 72)	Nonclinic Case (n = 53)
Shelter or safe housing program	4	0
Resource for financial assistance	28	21
Medical facility or provider	17	13
Counseling program or therapist	40**	15
Support group	14	17
Transportation resource	3	4*
Resource for crime-scene cleanup	3	0
Resource for obtaining a protective order or other type of protection	26	17

NOTE: * = $p < 0.05$. ** = $p < 0.01$.

who had clinic attorneys reported being referred to counseling, compared with 15 percent of victims without attorneys.

Summary

The victim survey yielded mixed results. Having a victims' rights attorney did lead to greater observance of some rights, according to victims surveyed. Specifically, victims who had attorneys were more likely to report that they were notified of defendants' release from jail, that they had made a VIS, and that they were notified of the case disposition. Also, victims who had attorneys were more likely to be referred to counseling services. However, victims who had attorneys were unexpectedly found to be less satisfied with the way they were treated by court officials, less satisfied with the court process, and less satisfied with the outcomes of their cases.

CHAPTER SIX

Community Impact

Community-level impacts of the clinics are probably the hardest to assess with some degree of rigor. We considered and rejected the idea of conducting community surveys as a second measure of community-level impact. Because there are no baseline community awareness measures, there is no good way to estimate change in awareness. (We do not think that community residents could reliably answer whether their awareness of victims' rights has changed since their state clinic opened.) Moreover, our experience in conducting research in this field suggested that public awareness of rights for victims is very low. Instead, we conducted an analysis of media content relating to victims' rights. Using the same time periods as the case-file samples, we searched state and local media in targeted jurisdictions to determine whether mention of victims' rights issues had increased since the local clinic started and whether the coverage of victims' rights stories had become more sympathetic to victims.

We used a methodology similar to one used by the principal investigator in an earlier NIJ project examining sources of public opinions of the police (Miller et al., 2005). We identified the major newspapers in each of the three states included in the impact research. Using the search capabilities in LexisNexis®, we located articles about victims' rights starting two years prior to the founding of the local clinic and going through the present time. We coded information from the articles captured to create several comparisons of the periods before and after the start-up of the victims' rights clinics within each of the three targeted states:

- number of articles mentioning victims' rights
- types of articles
- relevance of articles to victims' rights
- tone of articles (pro–victims' rights or neutral or anti–victims' rights).

There are well-documented dangers in relying on newspaper reports in social research. Lester (1980) argues that news workers filter events through a series of "news gates" created from values, norms, and rules that create templates against which events are measured for their newsworthiness. Oliver and Meyer (1999) found that multiple factors influenced what was considered newsworthy by the press, including event characteristics, news agency characteristics, and issue characteristics (especially those that resonate with social concerns).

Earl et al. (2004) categorize factors shaping news stories as either *selection bias* or *description bias*. *Selection bias* refers to the fact that newspapers cannot report all possible events and so need to pick and choose those that they do report. *Description bias* refers to the veracity or point of view contained in the stories that newspapers do report. Both of these forms of bias may have been reduced in our study by the fact that we relied on multiple sources. Moreover, because we were interested in change over time, both selection bias and description bias should have been relatively constant from one time period to the next.[1]

Methodology

Project staff identified all cities with a population of more than 75,000 in each of the three subject states, as well as the capital city of the state, even if that city had a lower population (as in Annapolis, Maryland). Using the Library of Congress's "Chronicling America" directory of newspapers, staff identified the major newspapers for each of those cities, as well as any statewide newspapers. That list of newspapers was then screened to determine whether their archives were available online either through LexisNexis or the newspaper's own website and extended back at least two years before the state's victims' rights clinic was established.

Using this system, the following newspapers were identified for inclusion:

- Maryland
  - *The Baltimore Sun*
  - *The Capital*
  - *Columbia Flier*
  - *The Daily Record*
  - *Maryland Gazette*
- South Carolina
  - *The Post and Courier*
  - *The State*
- Utah
  - *The Deseret News*
  - *Daily Herald*
  - *The Salt Lake Tribune.*

Articles were examined from two years prior to the founding of the legal clinics up through April 2010. Article archives were searched using the terms "victim and crime" or "victim and right" or "restitution." Articles identified under these broad terms were then reviewed individually by two NCVC attorneys to determine whether they contained a reference to a legal right of crime victims. This methodology resulted in a total collection of 647 Maryland articles, 288 South Carolina articles, and 358 Utah articles.

Project staff developed an assessment tool for newspaper articles. The tool allowed reviewers to identify the focus of the article (individual criminal case, legislation or policy, opinion, implementation of right, or a profile of an individual); indicate whether the article was "very" or "somewhat" relevant to victims' rights issues; whether the tone of the article was "supportive," "neutral," or "negative" toward victims' rights; and whether the article mentioned the victims' rights clinic or one of the clinic attorneys.

An article was considered to be "very" relevant if it explained or discussed the merit of a victim's right. For example, an article that talks about a victim's right to be heard during the

---

[1]   Of course, this would be true as long as newspaper staff and editorial policy remained constant from one time period to the next.

sentencing process in a death penalty case or one outlining what crime-related losses suffered by a victim are recoverable as restitution would be assessed as being "very" relevant. An article was "somewhat" relevant if it simply referenced a victim's right or mentioned a victim exercising or not exercising his or her right. Examples of "somewhat" relevant articles would include an article that reports only that the victim made a VIS or was not present in the courtroom during sentencing.

In determining the tone of the articles, an article that quotes several supporters of a right and little or no opposition—for example, an article on victims' rights–related legislation—is supportive. A profile of an individual that details his or her involvement in promoting victims' rights is also supportive because it reflects the paper's judgment that the person and victims' issues are worthy of public consideration. An article reporting the news in a factual manner that only mentions a victims' right or that a candidate running for office supports victims' rights without any more detail is neutral. If the writer takes a position on an issue, the article may be either supportive or negative, depending on the opinion reflected in the article.

The assessment tool was pilot tested on articles drawn from Arizona (a clinic state that is not a subject of this phase of the project) and refined. Three project staff rated each of the test articles independently and then compared notes. Cases in which there was disagreement were discussed and new criteria agreed upon. Then a second set of test articles was rated by the three staff independently. In the second ratings, agreement of all three raters was achieved in more than 70 percent of the articles reviewed for both the relevance and tone codings.

Each of the articles from Maryland, South Carolina, and Utah was coded independently by the three project staff using this scale. Where all three staff or two of the three staff assessments were in agreement, the consensus rating was used. In the rare instances in which all three staff differed in their assessment, staff met to discuss those articles and arrive at a consensus.

Types of Articles

Table 6.1 presents the results for type of article by state. The most common type of article by far in each of the states was articles about individual court cases. Typically, these articles were included because they made mention of VISs or excerpts of interviews with victims. Articles about individual cases constituted a majority of articles in Maryland and South Carolina and a plurality in Utah. In the other categories as well, states were relatively similar with some exceptions. Opinion articles—articles favoring or opposing victims' rights legislation or interpretation—made up 17 percent of the articles in Utah and 13 percent in South Carolina,

Table 6.1
Types of Articles, by State (%)

Article Type	Maryland (n = 645)	South Carolina (n = 288)	Utah (n = 357)
Individual case	62	52	45
Profile	4	8	10
Opinion	5	13	17
Legislation	18	9	15
Rights implementation	11	18	13

compared with just 5 percent in Maryland. Articles about the implementation of victims' rights comprised 18 percent of articles in South Carolina and 11 percent in Maryland and 13 percent of articles in Utah. The least common type of article across states was articles profiling individuals whose resume included work in the victims' rights area.

Number of Monthly Articles About Victims' Rights

Maryland

The clinic in Maryland was opened in April 2004. The articles that were examined were published between April 2002 and April 2010. During this time period, there were 645 articles total and 384 excluding articles about individual cases. The number of articles was grouped by month in order to determine the frequency, as shown in Figure 6.1.

The black vertical line represents the start of the clinic. A trend line fitted to show the overall trend of the monthly number of articles suggests that there was no change in the number of articles about victims' rights published before and after the Maryland clinic began. The visual trend line was confirmed by statistical testing: A two-group mean test compared the average number of articles per month before the clinic began and after the clinic began. According to the test, the preclinic mean of 6.75 articles per month was not significantly different from the postclinic mean of 6.58 articles per month.[2] In addition, a two-sided t-test to

Figure 6.1
Trends in Maryland Number of Articles per Month Relating to Victims' Rights

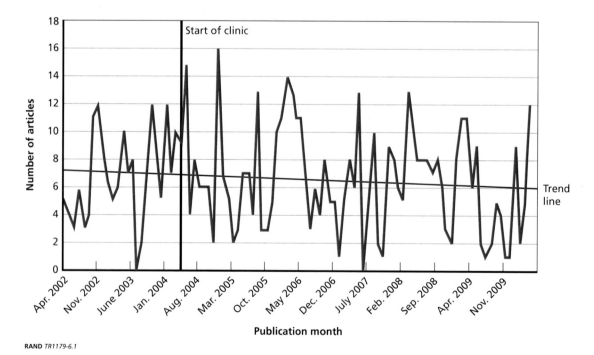

---

[2] $t[96] = 0.20$; $p = 0.84$.

determine whether the slope was nonzero was also conducted. The slope of the trend line did not significantly differ from zero, indicating no trend over time.[3]

South Carolina

The South Carolina clinic opened in April 2004. The articles examined in the study were published between April 2002 and March 2010. During this evaluation period, there were 287 total articles and 153 articles excluding articles about individual cases.

A trend line fitted to the monthly data displayed in Figure 6.2 showed a downward trend in the number of articles that referred to victims' rights that coincided closely with the opening of the victims' rights clinic. Although the number of articles per month picked up again in 2008, still the difference in mean number of articles per month—5.08 articles per month preclinic versus 2.29 articles per month postclinic—was statistically significant.[4] A test of the slope shows a negative and significant slope.[5]

Utah

The data range is from April 2003 to March 2010. During this time frame, there were 365 total articles. The monthly trend line for Utah was positive, indicating an increase in the monthly number of articles over time (see Figure 6.3). The difference in the mean number of articles preclinic (2.96 articles per month) versus postclinic (4.89 articles per month) was statistically

Figure 6.2
Trends in South Carolina Number of Articles per Month Relating to Victims' Rights

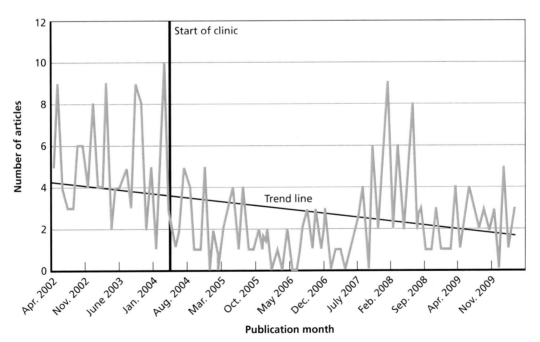

RAND *TR1179-6.2*

---

[3] $t[95] = -0.95$; $p = 0.343$.

[4] $t[95] = 5.74$; $p < 0.01$.

[5] $t[95] = -3.19$; $p = 0.002$.

Figure 6.3
Trends in Utah Number of Articles per Month Relating to Victims' Rights

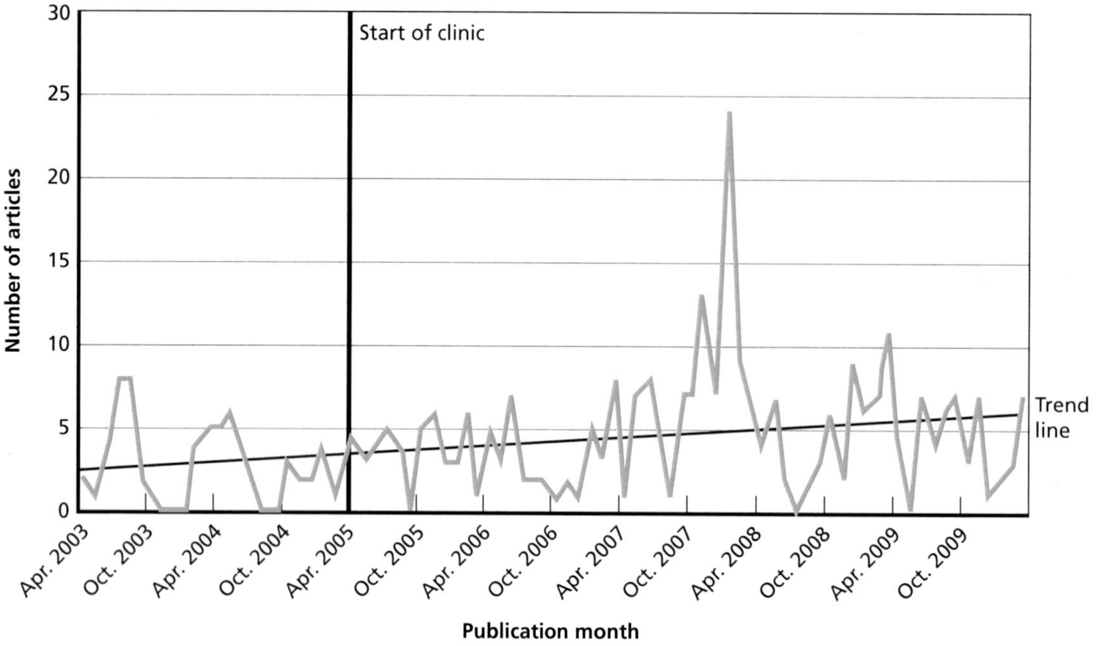

significant.[6] The test of the slope was also significant and positive.[7] Much of the pre- versus postclinic difference in the number of articles is due to a spike in articles in January 2008, when 18 separate news articles related to a mass shooting in Trolley Square.

We also compared the frequency of articles before and after the clinics opened using a second measure. Many of the articles contained news about individual cases, the number of which we thought would be less affected by presence of a victims' rights clinic than the number of other types of articles. A second measure, therefore, was the number of articles before versus after the clinics started, excluding those articles that were only about individual cases. We also constructed a third measure, the number of articles *highly relevant* to victims' rights issues excluding articles about individual cases. This last set of articles is where we would expect the presence of a victims' rights clinic to have the greatest impact.

The results of these latter two sets of tests are presented in Table 6.2. The trends over time in these measures simply confirm the pattern that we saw above for all articles about victims' rights. That is, in Maryland, there was no change in frequency coincident with opening of the victims' rights clinic; in South Carolina, there was a decline in frequency; in Utah, there was an increase in frequency.

---

[6] $t[83] = -2.41$; $p < 0.01$.

[7] $t[95] = 2.67$; $p = 0.002$.

Table 6.2
Mean Number of Monthly Articles About Victims' Rights Pre- and Postclinic in Three States

State	Articles Excepting Those About Individual Court Cases		Highly Relevant Articles Excepting Those About Individual Court Cases	
	Preclinic	Postclinic	Preclinic	Postclinic
Maryland	3.96	4.11	2.27	2.09
South Carolina	2.67	1.91*	1.67	1.26
Utah	2.00	2.69*	1.67	2.42

NOTE: * = p < 0.05.

Tone of Articles

The tone of the articles was evaluated to determine whether the opening of the clinic had an effect on the way in which victims' rights were portrayed. When the tone of the article was compared for pre- and postclinic Maryland articles, 77 percent of the preclinic articles were supportive versus 75 percent after the clinic opened. The difference was not significant (p = 0.627).[8] In South Carolina, 16 percent of the articles were coded as supportive prior to the clinic opening, and 17 percent of the articles were supportive after the clinic opened. Again, this slight difference did not approach statistical significance.[9] A similar result was observed in Utah, where 38 percent of the articles were judged to be supportive prior to the start of the clinic, compared with 35 percent after the clinic opened.[10] See Table 6.3.

We also note that there were substantial differences between the states in the extent to which articles were sympathetic to victims' rights. Maryland, which has a long history of victims' rights, had by far the highest rate of sympathetic articles: about three in four. Utah, also a strong, but more recent, victims' rights state, had the next-highest rate of sympathetic articles (a little better than one in three). South Carolina, with the weakest tradition of victims' rights, had the smallest proportion of sympathetic articles (about one in six).

Table 6.3
Changes in the Proportion of Articles Supportive of Victims' Rights (%)

State	Preclinic	Postclinic
Maryland	77	75
South Carolina	16	17
Utah	38	35

[8] Chi-square [1] = 0.24; p = 0.63.

[9] Chi-square [1] = 0.06; p = 0.81.

[10] Chi-square [1] = 0.13; p = 0.72.

Mentions of Clinics and Clinic Attorneys

Maryland also had the highest rate of clinics and clinic attorneys cited in articles: About one in six cases cited the victims' rights clinic or clinic attorney (see Table 6.4). The victims' rights clinic was cited in about one in ten Utah articles, and a clinic was cited in 3 percent of articles. In South Carolina, the victims' rights clinic or clinic attorneys were cited in 4 percent of articles reviewed.

Summary

When we examine the media coverage across the three states, we see overall that the opening of the clinics did not coincide with more-frequent or more-sympathetic coverage of victims' rights in the print media. We did observe a significant increase in the number of victims' rights articles in Utah but actually a decline in the number of articles in South Carolina. In Maryland, there was no change, but that is not unexpected because the primary clinic attorney had been involved in victims' rights work long before the clinic began as a separate entity. We did not observe a change in the proportion of articles sympathetic to victims' rights in any of the three states. The clinics and clinic attorneys were most in the news in Maryland, least in South Carolina.

Table 6.4
Attorney or Clinic Cited in the Articles
Post–Clinic Opening (%)

State	Attorney Cited	Clinic Cited
Maryland	16	17
South Carolina	4	4
Utah	9	3

CHAPTER SEVEN

Clinics' Impact on the Legal Landscape

Legal rights for crime victims have been developed and expanded during the past three decades. These rights have transformed the relationship between the crime victim and the criminal justice system as victims gained the rights to be informed, present, and heard during the criminal and juvenile justice processes. This change has been driven largely by crime victims and survivors, with the support of advocacy organizations, leaders in the criminal justice field, and policymakers. Despite this remarkable progress in the passage of crime victims' rights, few states—even those that have adopted constitutional amendments—provide recourse to victims when their rights are not honored. The clinics were conceived as a response to the fact that many victims still are not receiving the rights they are formally granted under the law and are intended to promote awareness, education, and enforcement of crime victims' rights in the criminal justice system.

We attempted to measure the impact of each clinic's work on the legal landscape of its state by examining new and amended victims' rights legislation and court decisions interpreting those rights for the two years preceding the establishment of each clinic through the end of 2010. A review of new and amended statutes and court rules allows us to examine the legislative climate and trends surrounding victims' rights in each of the target states before and after the clinics were established. It also provides an opportunity to evaluate whether the hands-on work done by the clinics to help victims ensure that their rights are respected in a real-world setting also helps highlight statutory deficiencies that support the need for legislative change.

The case law analysis, comparing the number and content of published opinions on victims' rights at the trial and appellate levels throughout the state, provides a comparison of victims' rights case law before and after implementation of the clinics in each of the target states. The number of appellate cases considering crime victims' rights may indicate the willingness of the judiciary to give meaningful consideration to those rights, especially when the appeal is brought by the victim or on the victim's behalf. Such cases also provide an indication of the acceptance of victims' standing to assert their rights. Analysis of those opinions reflects the development of case law interpreting the statutory rights of victims.

Statutory Analysis

The statutory analysis conducted during this part of the project was an extension of the analysis that was started during phase 1 of the project. During phase 1, legal provisions relating to victims' rights, including statutes and court rules, were reviewed for any substantive changes since the formation of the clinic in each of the targeted states for the following issues of victims' rights:

- the right to be informed
- the right to attend court proceedings
- the right to be heard
- the right to protection
- the right to privacy
- the right to victim compensation
- the right to restitution
- the right to a speedy trial
- the right to return of property
- enforcement of victims' rights.

The initial collection covered the years 2004 through 2008 for Maryland and South Carolina and the years 2005 through 2008 for Utah. Substantive amendments and new laws enacted during the applicable time period were identified and summarized. For any new or substantively amended provisions identified, project staff attempted to determine any connection to the legal clinic.[1] Often, the work of a clinic may demonstrate the need for legislation. If the clinic loses a case or is unable to help a victim because of barriers or defects in the system, this failure helps to make the case for a legislative solution. In other cases, a clinic's parent organization works to support legislation that strengthens victims' rights or is of interest to crime victims.

Changes to statutes and court rules that affect crime victims' rights were collected and summarized for the two-year period preceding the federal funding of the clinic, as well as changes that took place after the initial collection from phase 1 of the project. New victims' rights statutes and court rules enacted in 2009 and 2010 were also reviewed. Although statutes and court rules serve different purposes and the process for enacting statutes varies from the process for adopting court rules, project staff did not feel the need to analyze the two separately. In most instances, the court rules followed the passage of the statutes and were adopted to reinforce or clarify the statutory rights of crime victims.

Figure 7.1 depicts the average annual numbers of pre- and postclinic statutes and court rules identified for each target state. For Maryland, 31 applicable statutes and court rules were identified for the preclinic period (15.5 per year) and 63 postclinic (nine per year). For South Carolina, we identified 16 preclinic statutes and rules (eight per year) and 52 postclinic statutes and court rules (7.5 per year). For Utah, we found 29 preclinic statutes and court rules (14.5 per year) and 54 postclinic (nine per year). The decline in the number of amended or newly enacted victim-related legislation per year is not surprising because most of the victims' rights legislation is initially passed to implement each state's constitutional victims' rights amendment and thereafter only to fill any gaps or to clarify procedures to be followed when affording victims their rights.

Each clinic reported involvement in support of some legislation passed during the postclinic period. The Maryland clinic was involved in 37 percent of the legislation, South Carolina

---

[1]   The clinics do not use any federal funds to lobby for legislation. All legislative advocacy is conducted by individuals on their own time or using nonfederal funding.

Figure 7.1
Annual Number of Statutes and Court Rules per State

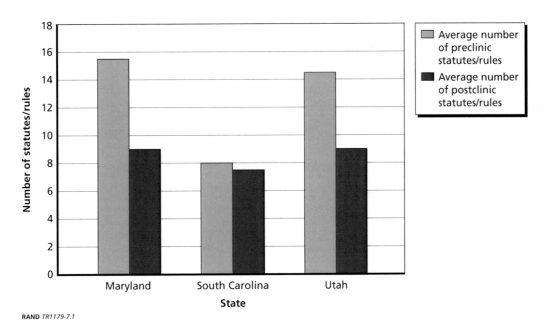

RAND *TR1179-7.1*

69 percent, and Utah 6 percent. However, "involvement" by the clinics ranges from signing on to a letter of support with other organizations to much more in-depth advocacy by a clinic's parent organization.

More important than the number of statutes is the statutes' effect on the expansion of victims' rights. To create measures of the impact of legislation, each of the statutes or court rules was independently coded by two project attorneys based on the following metrics to measure the impact of the statutes on the expansion of victims' rights in each of the states:

- How does the change affect the number of victims given protection? (fewer, neutral, more)
- How does the change affect the enforceability of the law? (limits, neutral, expands)
- How does the change affect the scope of victims' rights? (add a new right, take one away, shrink or expand an existing right)
- Does the change improve how the law is implemented? (impairs, neutral, improves)
- What was the relationship of the change to the clinic's work? (backlash against clinic work or clinic proved need for victim protection)

Table 7.1 summarizes the positive impacts found when these performance metrics were applied in the analysis of the statute and court rule changes during the pre- and postclinic periods. The table shows that postclinic statutes and court rules had positive impacts 10 or more percentage points greater than preclinic statutes and court rules in two of the five impact categories in Maryland (increases number of victims affected and expands scope of right), in two of five categories in Utah (expands enforceability and improves implementation of right), and in none of the five in South Carolina. In contrast, positive impacts were 10 percentage points or more greater among preclinic statutes and court rules in two impact categories in

Table 7.1
Percentage of Statutes and Court Rules with Positive Impact

Effect	Preclinic	Postclinic
Maryland		
Increases number of victims affected	2	3
Expands enforceability	2	5
Expands scope of right	2	9
Improves implementation of right	8	8
Direct connection to clinic work	0	7
South Carolina		
Increases number of victims affected	3	9
Expands enforceability	6	4
Expands scope of right	3	9
Improves implementation of right	9	3
Direct connection to clinic work	0	9
Utah		
Increases number of victims affected	5	6
Expands enforceability	4	0
Expands scope of right	5	4
Improves implementation of right	5	7
Direct connection to clinic work	0	6

South Carolina (increases number of victims affected, improves implementation of right), in one impact category in Utah (increases number of victims affected), and none in Maryland.

Case Law Analysis

Case law analysis also began during phase 1 of this project. As each of the statutes and court rules was checked for amendments, the case annotations provided in LexisNexis were also reviewed for any relevant court decisions interpreting the statute or rule handed down during the applicable time period. Each case was summarized, and project staff attempted to determine any connection with the case to the legal clinic.

Relevant victim-related court decisions for the three target states were identified and summarized for the two-year period preceding federal funding for the clinics and for those issued since the initial collection of case law during phase 1 of the project. For Maryland, 189 cases were reviewed; 107 cases were reviewed for South Carolina; and 79 cases were reviewed for Utah. Including the cases that were identified and summarized in phase 1 of the project, for Maryland, five applicable cases were identified for the preclinic period and 24 postclinic, or a total of 29 court decisions that were analyzed. For South Carolina, two preclinic and ten postclinic cases, or a total of 12, were analyzed. One of these South Carolina cases was not officially published. For Utah, nine preclinic and 17 postclinic cases, or a total of 26, were analyzed. Seven of the Utah cases were not officially published. Figure 7.2 reflects the average number of pre- and postclinic cases identified for each target state.

We observed modest increases in the annual number of appellate decisions on victims' rights following the opening of the clinics in Maryland and South Carolina. In Maryland and South Carolina, the number of decisions went up after the clinics began, from 2.5 per year to 3.4 per year in Maryland and from one per year to 1.5 per year in South Carolina. However, in Utah, the number declined following the opening of the clinic there, from 4.5 per year to 2.8 per year. Each clinic's involvement in cases was determined for the period that the clinic was in operation. The Maryland clinic was involved in 33 percent of the postclinic cases, South Carolina in 20 percent, and Utah in 12 percent.

As with statutes, not only the number of appellate decisions is important but also how those decisions affect the practice of victims' rights law. To create measures of the impact of court decisions, each of the court decisions was independently coded by two project attorneys based on the following metrics to measure the impact of the clinics on case law change:

- Was the clinic involved in the case? (Y/N)
- Do other cases cite the decision for its holding on a victims' rights issue? (Y/N)
- Is there a law review article analyzing the decision? (Y/N)
- Did the decision result in legislative or policy change? (Y/N)
- Did the decision challenge a long-established interpretation of the law (for example, right to give victim-impact testimony in death-penalty cases)? (Y/N)
- Did the decision expand a victim's right? (Y/N)
- Does the decision mandate certain action, or was it a permissive ruling? (Y/N)
- Does the decision have the potential for affecting a significant number of victims? (Y/N)

Figure 7.2
Average Number of Cases per Year

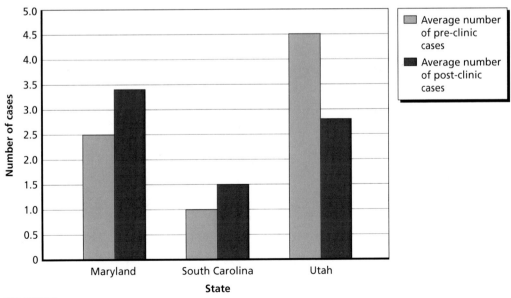

The results show that postclinic appellate cases had greater impacts in the postclinic period (at least 10 percentage points greater than in the preclinic period) for five of the eight categories in both Maryland and Utah (for Maryland: case cited in other decisions, case challenged long-standing interpretation, case expanded right, case resulted in mandatory action, and case affected significant number of victims; for Utah: case cited in other decisions, case subject of law review article, case expanded right, case limited right, and case affected significant number of victims) and in two of the eight categories in South Carolina (case cited in other decisions and case expanded right) (see Table 7.2). Impacts were substantially greater in the preclinic period in just one category in Maryland and Utah (case cited in other decisions and mandatory actions, respectively) and in two in South Carolina (case cited in other decisions and case subject of law review article).

We also found that, in two of the states, there was a significant increase in the number of court decisions that limited the right, from 20 percent of cases preclinic to 50 percent postclinic in Maryland and from 11 percent preclinic to 29 percent postclinic in Utah. This is not surprising, given that the clinics were attempting to aggressively promote the rights of victims and expected to lose some of the cases. South Carolina, which did not employ such an aggressive approach, saw fewer cases limiting the rights of victims, from 50 percent preclinic to only 10 percent postclinic.

Examples of Promoting Victims' Rights Through Legislation and Court Decisions

The following are some examples of legislative changes and court decisions through which the clinics have affected the legal landscape of each of the target states.

In Maryland, some of the legal changes were directly related to the work of the clinic. A prime example is the 2006 legislation giving victims of juveniles the ability to seek an appeal when their rights are violated. A pro bono clinic attorney had represented a victim of a juvenile who had attempted to appeal a denial of rights, but the court had ruled in 2005 that victims of juvenile offenders could not exercise the right to seek appeal. That pro bono attorney became a state legislator and was responsible for the 2006 amendment extending the right to victims of juveniles.

South Carolina has an active advocacy network that has worked to strengthen victims' rights. This progress has continued through the recent years the legal clinic has been in operation. In 2008, South Carolina provided for victim notification and the right to be heard when an offender seeks postconviction DNA testing. Although the clinic itself was not involved in these legislative changes, its parent organization, the South Carolina Victim Assistance Network, publicly supported many of the changes.

Utah also continued to expand its legal rights for victims during the period of the clinic's existence. In 2007, Utah amended a court rule to provide safeguards for victims when their records are subpoenaed, requiring that, before such records can be requested, the court must first hold a hearing and determine that the defendant is entitled to such records. Clinic staff were asked their opinions regarding the need for the rule change; however, they were not the advocates for that change. In 2008, Utah gave victims the right to submit a written statement in any action on appeal that is related to the crime committed against the victim. Two clinic

Table 7.2
Percentage of Cases in Which Appellate Decisions Had Positive Impact

Effect	Preclinic		Postclinic	
	Percentage	Observations	Percentage	Observations
Maryland				
Case cited in other court decisions	80	4	58	1
Case subject of law review article	0		8	2
Case generated legislative or policy change	20	1	17	4
Case challenged long-established interpretation	0		13	3
Case expanded right	0		21	5
Mandatory action as opposed to permissive ruling	40	2	58	14
Case affected significant number of victims	60	3	71	17
South Carolina				
Case cited in other court decisions	50	1	40	4
Case subject of law review article	50	1	10	1
Case generated legislative or policy change	0		0	
Case challenged long-established interpretation	0		0	
Case expanded right	0		40	4
Mandatory action as opposed to permissive ruling	0		0	
Case affected significant number of victims	50	1	50	1
Utah				
Case cited in other court decisions	33	3	53	9
Case subject of law review article	22	2	58	10
Case generated legislative or policy change	0		0	
Case challenged long-established interpretation	0		0	
Case expanded right	11	1	24	4
Mandatory action as opposed to permissive ruling	22	2	12	2
Case affected significant number of victims	33	3	53	9

clients testified on legislation to give victims the right to submit a written statement on any appeal related to the crime.

Case law regarding crime victims' rights has also developed during the time the clinics have been funded. In 2008, the Maryland Court of Appeals ruled on two cases involving victims' rights. In the first and most significant, the court found that crime victims and their attorneys had standing to participate in an appeal. However, the court noted that "there remains no effective tangible remedy for a victim to seek to 'un-do' what already has been done in a criminal case." In that case, the victim was not notified of hearings reconsidering the sentence of her assailant and, thus, was denied her right to be heard at those hearings (*Hoile v.*

State, 404 Md. 591, 948 A. 2d 30 [2008]). In another case, the court held that a broad defini-tion of *crime victim* applied to the victim compensation law (*Opert v. Criminal Injuries Comp. Bd.*, 403 Md. 587, 943 A. 2d 1229 [Md. Ct. App. 2008]). The Maryland clinic represented the victims in each of the above cases involving crime-victim standing or remedies for a viola-tion of rights and provided assistance to the victim's counsel in the case of *Opert v. Criminal Injuries Comp. Bd.*

In 2007, the South Carolina Supreme Court found that victims entitled to receive resti-tution from offenders, among others, had no private right of action against the Department of Corrections for improperly diverting the offenders' wages into a department surplus fund (*Tor-rence v. S.C. Dept. of Corr.*, 646 S.E. 2d 866 [S.C. 2007]). Although the clinic had no direct involvement in this case, the clinic's parent organization filed an amicus brief in the case.

In 2008, the Utah Court of Appeals affirmed a trial court's decision granting a defen-dant's motion for an in camera inspection of the victim's mental-health records. The case was appealed to the Utah Supreme Court, and the clinic filed an amicus brief arguing that the Court of Appeals violated Utah Code § 77-38-11, which requires the court to rule on all prop-erly presented issues, when it failed to address whether victims' rights protections should or must be considered when examining exceptions to the victim's psychotherapist-patient privi-lege. The Supreme Court found that this section did not apply because the Court of Appeals did not make any adverse ruling upon which to rest a claim for injunctive relief, declaratory relief, or a writ of mandamus or of a motion or request brought by the victim of a crime. Vic-tims' rights were not addressed on appeal because the issue "was not properly presented for appeal to the Court of Appeals" (*State v. Worthen*, 222 P. 3d 1144 [Utah 2009]).

Summary

We observed a decrease in the annual number of victims' rights statutes and court rules in each of the three states following introduction of the clinics. Given that each of these states had already passed significant victims' rights legislation prior to the opening of the clinics (and, in fact, that may have been one of the reasons that these states were chosen to have clinics), this is not surprising. We found evidence that clinic attorneys did play a role in most of the legisla-tion in South Carolina and a good portion of the legislation in Maryland. We also found some indication that statutes enacted postclinic had greater positive impact on the expansion of vic-tims' rights, especially in Maryland.

There were modest increases in the annual number of appellate cases in Maryland and South Carolina (but not in Utah). Clinic attorneys were involved in a small proportion of these cases in each state. Measures of the decisions' impact indicated that cases decided following the opening of the clinics, particularly in Maryland and Utah, had greater impact.

CHAPTER EIGHT
Clinic Sustainability

From the beginning, the victims' rights clinics have faced challenges in finding the funds to sustain their work. The original intent of the federal demonstration grant was to develop proof of concept so that other sources of funding could be found and potential funders convinced of the value of the model. The clinics have struggled, using primarily federal funds to cover costs longer than originally intended. But, in the current climate of austerity, the continuation of federal funding is uncertain.

Grant Funding

All clinics have relied on federal grant funding, principally that received through NCVLI. The crime victims' rights clinics were initially funded through NCVLI for three years of activity. That funding has been continued. In addition, each clinic has been able to supplement that funding with additional grants. Maryland has been the most successful in diversifying its funding: It has received a VOCA assistance grant; an Edward Byrne Memorial Justice Assistance Grant; a Services, Training, Officers, and Prosecutors (STOP) Violence Against Women Grant; and a grant from the state for legal services. South Carolina received a grant from that state's bar association's foundation, and Utah received a VOCA assistance grant.

Although federal grant funding has been the lifeblood of the clinics, it is not without its challenges. There are often delays in receiving grant funding. A state grant administrator may not fund the same project two years in a row. The grants are often limited to 12 months, making it difficult to retain services and key staff. Moreover, grant funding sources are not uniformly available to all clinics. For example, the Utah clinic does not qualify for its state bar foundation grants. In addition to the grants identified above, several clinics have expressed interest in seeking funding for a Legal Assistance for Victims Grant from the Office on Violence Against Women.

All three clinics have sought funding from private foundations, but only South Carolina has been successful. According to the clinic directors and NCVLI's executive director, the biggest obstacle has been the difficulty in explaining the need for the clinics. Private funders often assume that the prosecutor will enforce the rights of victims and do not understand the role of a victim's attorney. Utah faces another particular barrier: Private foundations will not consider an applicant that has not undergone an audit, but, for a small organization like the clinic, an audit is a significant expense.

Leveraging Existing Funding

Each of the three clinics has leveraged its grant funding in some way. The Maryland and South Carolina clinics are programs within larger organizations through which they have office space and equipment. Utah, too, received office space and access to equipment from a larger organization, the Rape Recovery Center, for the first several years of its existence. It recently outgrew the space and moved into its own offices.

The clinics have also been able to utilize volunteers, interns, and pro bono attorneys to varying degrees. Utah has made the largest use of interns, using a close working relationship with two law schools to recruit 12 to 18 legal interns per year. Those interns conduct intake, court accompaniment, legal research, and other duties. Maryland also uses legal interns during the summer and has been able to use other volunteers for such tasks as cleaning up its database. It currently has a social work intern who, although technically working for the larger organization, helps with client intake.

The use of pro bono attorneys varies between the clinics. South Carolina has made the greatest use, with 14 pro bono attorneys providing assistance in emergencies and when cases are at a distance from the clinic's offices. Utah uses pro bono attorneys in the same situations. Maryland reports that its use of pro bono attorneys is primarily as local counsel in federal cases outside of Maryland and to represent victims in collateral civil matters, such as landlord/tenant disputes or handling a victim's estate. For criminal case work, the clinic director believes that it takes too much effort to support pro bono attorneys, who often lack experience in criminal law and victims' rights. The director notes that, even when it has a talented attorney, a case often involves pretrial motions and hearings; the trial; postconviction proceedings, including the sentencing; and, often, an appeal. Many of the issues raised are substantive and time-intensive. As a result, the cases generally consume more time than the attorney expected, making him or her reluctant to take a second case. A principal complication for the use of pro bono attorneys is that victims' rights representation is a new area of law. There is not a "road map" for action. Other players in the criminal case are not sure how to treat a victim's attorney. Representation requires an ability to assert oneself confidently in an area in which procedures are not yet standard. The Maryland clinic director and NCVLI's executive director expressed the opinion that, once this area of law is more settled, the use of pro bono attorneys will become more feasible.

Donations and Other Support

Along with securing grants, the clinics have tried to identify or create other sources of support. Unfortunately, none of the clinics has yet been able to secure a substantial amount of donations to support its operations. NCVLI notes that this is partly a problem of a lack of time and lack of expertise in fundraising by the clinic directors.

The clinic directors discussed other possible funding sources, including crime-victim compensation programs, which already pay many of the out-of-pocket expenses of crime victims as prescribed by state statute. All were aware that New Jersey had changed its law to allow victim compensation to reimburse victims for their attorney fees, but they did not believe they could get such a change in their own states. Maryland and Utah directors both mentioned that crime-victim compensation programs in their states had cut back benefits recently and had funding problems, so amending the compensation law to add attorneys' fees did not seem like the right avenue to pursue at present.

Maryland has been successful in working with its legislature to create an additional funding source for crime-victim legal services, providing that unclaimed victim restitution would be deposited into a fund to support legal services for victims. However, the legislation provided that such funding would be awarded through a grant process, and another organization was the successful applicant for the first two years the funding was available. The clinic did receive funds in the most recent year, but the director noted that the amount of funding available through this source varies quite a bit from year to year. Maryland also tried to create another funding source this past year by adding a court cost. But the legislation, which named the Maryland Crime Victims' Resource Center as the recipient, was opposed by some other victim organizations, and the bill was defeated.

Each of the clinic directors was asked whether he or she would consider charging for his or her services. They all agreed they might have to look at such a system of operation but were reluctant to do so. Maryland noted that a previous proposal to tap into victim insurance to pay for the work of the organization's social worker had been soundly rejected by the organization's board, so it did not think that the board would support charging victims for services.

The South Carolina director also pointed to the another funding approach pioneered by the New Jersey clinic, in which attorneys representing victims in a civil case related to the offense also represent their interests in the criminal case for no additional fee. Although it requires attorneys who are comfortable representing victims in both the civil and criminal arenas, the South Carolina clinic director believed it to be a sustainable approach to victim representation in cases with viable civil claims. The director of the New Jersey clinic agrees, with an important caveat: This approach requires a level of initial funding or affiliation with an established firm that can support the victim practice. Crime-victim cases are typically tort cases, which are generally taken on a contingency-fee basis (i.e., the attorney does not get paid for his or her time but instead receives a percentage of any settlement or judgment if the case is successful). Such cases can take several years to come to judgment and collection, so there must be some form of ongoing financial support to sustain the work of the victims' attorneys until the civil practice starts to thrive.

Raising the Profile of Clinics

The clinic directors were asked about their efforts to raise their profiles, which could help garner support from the public or funders. The Maryland director noted that his program was trying to connect better with supporters, with a monthly e-blast by the larger organization going to 4,000–5,000 people that includes highlights of the clinic's work. The larger organization also uses social media, including a blog, two Facebook pages, a LinkedIn account, and Twitter. Maryland also noted that it had many media contacts with which it had built good relationships over the years. It recognized that it could do more press releases to raise awareness but lacked time and staff expertise. Also, this type of outreach is not currently funded.

The Utah clinic noted that it raises awareness through regular interaction with the state-wide victims' advocate organization. In addition, a staffer serves on the Utah Council on Victims of Crime, so it stays informed of clinic activities. And one of its attorneys has been asked to join the state's coalition against domestic violence.

Utah also reports good relations with the media. It has been featured multiple times in the past year. However, it does not have a formal media plan. In South Carolina, the parent organization is the network of state victim advocates, so its clinic has a built-in mechanism for promotion.

Outlook for Sustainability

Clinic directors were asked about their outlook for two years from now. The Maryland clinic director is confident the clinic will still exist but probably as a smaller operation. The Utah director characterized herself as "cautiously optimistic" that it will still be in existence. And the South Carolina director was making long-range plans with the United Way to become sustainable.

But aside from their own clinics, their outlook for victims' rights clinics, generally, was pessimistic. The Maryland director noted that, although the clinics were authorized under the federal Justice for All Act (Pub. L. 108-405, 2004), they had never been included in the president's budget proposal. Advocates' ability to get funding appropriated by Congress for a program not included in the president's budget is very limited, especially since the reduction of earmarks. So the clinic directors and NCVLI felt that it was unlikely the full network of clinics could be maintained, which would mean a loss of the structure that allows clinic directors and attorneys to interact, problem-solve, and share knowledge and experiences.

CHAPTER NINE
Conclusions

When we began the impact evaluation, we acknowledged the difficulty in finding measurable effects of the victims' rights clinics. The diverse set of effects that the clinics were trying to bring about—changes in attitudes toward victims' rights among criminal justice officials but also in the larger community, increasing compliance with victims' rights, establishing legal precedence for victims' rights, and aiding individuals in navigating the justice process—required that we capture a range of measures in multiple sites. We had no benchmarks on which to draw in looking at attitudinal change because the evaluation was funded well after most of the clinics began work. The work establishing legal precedents is especially difficult to assess quantitatively because just one published appellate opinion, statute, or even court rule may have a profound effect on the enforcement of rights of victims.

To assess effects on the attitudes of court officials, we used pre- and postclinic surveys of court officials in Colorado and retrospective surveys in the three states with established clinics. Survey results indicated a shift toward more-favorable attitudes toward victims' rights and greater compliance by court officials. The attitudinal changes were small but consistent within each professional group—prosecutors, victim advocates, and judges. (In contrast, defense attorneys in each state said that their opinions about victims' rights had become more negative over time.) We observed larger shifts when asking about compliance with victims' rights, this time among all professional groups, including defense attorneys. The simple pre-post or post-test-only designs that we used cannot establish whether the shift in attitudes and compliance resulted wholly or partially from the work of the clinics. We can say that the observed changes are consistent with the stated purpose of the clinics.

Measuring clinic effects on community attitudes toward victims' rights, we faced the same problem of having no preclinic data to serve as a benchmark. Partly for this reason and partly because we thought it likely that most members of the general public would be at best minimally aware of victims' rights and the work of the clinics, we decided not to survey the general public. Instead, we examined coverage of victims' rights in the print media, where we would be able to use archives to compare pre- and postclinic coverage. We found an increase in the number of articles about victims' rights in one state (Utah) but no change in Maryland and a decline in South Carolina. We did not observe a change in the proportion of articles sympathetic to victims' rights in any of the three states. Coverage of the clinics and clinic attorneys was most prevalent in Maryland, least in South Carolina.

The evaluation contained two measures of actual compliance with victims' rights to check on the self-descriptions of behavior provided by court officials in the surveys. One measure was derived from records of victims' rights in seven prosecutors' offices that handled the bulk of clinic cases in Maryland, South Carolina, and Utah. Gathering these data proved to be difficult because, in general, we found the information on compliance in prosecutor files to be poorly organized and incomplete. When we did manage to assemble the data, we found significant differences in compliance on some measures in some sites. Nonetheless, we did not find an overall effect on compliance of having a victims' rights attorney. However, we did find that, across sites, cases in which victims had attorneys were less likely to be dismissed and more likely to result in convictions than cases without a victims' rights attorney.

The poor state of records kept on compliance with victims' rights likely reflects the fact that victims' rights statutes do not contain enforcement mechanisms: There are no clear consequences for court officials when victims are denied their rights, so there is no compelling reason to track compliance. Being able to track compliance accurately is a first step in ensuring that victims' rights are honored. As the Maryland clinic director told us, "What gets counted is what gets done."

In contrast to the results of the case-file analysis, when we interviewed victims, we found that having a victims' rights attorney led to greater observance of some rights, according to those surveyed. Victims represented by clinic attorneys more often reported that they were notified of defendants' release from jail, that they had made a VIS, and that they were notified of the case disposition. Victims who had an attorney were more likely to be referred to counseling services. However, contrary to expectations, victims represented by clinic attorneys were less satisfied with the way they were treated by court officials, less satisfied with the court process, and less satisfied with the outcome of their case.

We suspect that the reason for lower satisfaction with the court process among victims represented by clinic attorneys is that victims who sought out attorneys were already dissatisfied with their treatment in the criminal justice system. An alternative explanation is that the clinic attorneys increased victims' awareness of their rights and of what might be achieved through prosecution but then victims were disappointed by what actually happened in court.

We found some evidence that clinics made a difference in the expansion of victims' rights. Overall, we did not observe changes in the annual number of statutes and court rules following the opening of the clinics. However, clinic attorneys did play a role in enacting most of the legislation in South Carolina and a good portion of the legislation in Maryland. We also found limited evidence that statutes enacted postclinic had greater positive impact on the expansion of victims' rights, especially in Maryland.

We observed that there were modest increases in the annual number of appellate cases in Maryland and South Carolina (but not in Utah). However, clinic attorneys were involved in a small proportion of these cases in each state. Particularly in Maryland and Utah, we found, on measures of the impact of the decisions, a greater effect of published rulings following the opening of the clinics.

Final Thoughts

The results of the impact evaluation indicate that victims' rights clinics can make a difference in promoting the rights of victims in individual cases; they may help more generally to promote a more sympathetic view of victims' rights among court officials; and they have had some influence in expanding the rights of victims in the states where they reside through their involvement in influential appellate decisions and legislative efforts. According to these results, the demonstration project was, on balance, successful.

The policy question now is how to build on the experience of the demonstration project to ensure that victims' rights are honored in the criminal justice process. The demonstration placed clinics in only a small number of states; the clinics are in just one location in those states; and, even in those locations, they serve only a handful of victims. As providers of services to individual victims, clinics are resource-intensive, raising questions about whether they could ever be built out sufficiently to provide services to a significant proportion of victims. One way forward would be to create an expanded set of clinics making up one part of a comprehensive effort to ensure that victims' rights are honored. Another component could include wide-scale use of pro bono attorneys or law school clinics, a model much less costly than the NCVLI clinics staffed with dedicated attorneys. NCVLI could play a role in educating attorneys and students in victim law. A third component could include the creation or expansion of the role of state victim ombudsmen with power to sanction agencies that exhibited a pattern of failure to comply with victims' rights requirements.

There are significant problems with both use of pro bono attorneys and victim ombudsmen. It can be argued that, even if a statewide network of pro bono attorneys could be recruited and maintained, the attorneys would lack the expertise of dedicated victims' rights attorneys. Moreover, if cases require more time than expected, pro bono attorneys might not have the time needed to dedicate to their assigned victims' rights cases. Law clinic students graduate and may terminate their involvement in a case before it is decided or before rights issues have been resolved. Victim ombudsmen are likely to get involved only after someone's rights have been violated, when it may be too late to help that individual. These are valid criticisms, and, for these reasons, NCVLI's director does not favor this approach. But our earlier process evaluation finds that some of the clinics made successful use of pro bono attorneys in well-defined situations. Moreover, widespread protection of the rights of individual victims may be achievable only by using a model that is far less expensive than providing funding for a network of dedicated victims' rights attorneys that has true statewide or national coverage.

In this model, victims' rights clinics would do what they are best equipped to do: fight for victim standing in court and, in other ways, work to expand victims' rights through appellate and legislative work. With this focused approach, clinics could be situated at the state level, the regional level, or even consolidated at the national level, depending on the availability and amount of funding. This model would continue to grow the body of victims' rights case law and may, as issues are defined and narrowed, make pro bono or law clinic representation of victims at the trial court level more feasible in the future.

APPENDIX A
Survey for Colorado Criminal Justice Officials

This appendix reproduces the Survey of Criminal Justice Professionals on Victims' Rights.

Survey of Criminal Justice Professionals on Victims' Rights

Purpose: The purpose of the survey is to gather information about the knowledge, attitudes, and behavior of criminal justice professionals with regard to crime victims' rights. These responses, as a group, will be compared with responses to a similar post-test to be conducted in about a year, to measure any change that takes place during that year. The survey is part of a larger effort to evaluate the impact of crime victims' rights legal clinics in several states.

Voluntary: Your participation in this survey is completely voluntary. You may leave any question blank and stop at any time. Your employment, affiliations, and standing in any group or association will in no way be affected by your participation or non-participation in the survey.

Confidential: All survey responses are confidential, and your identity will never be revealed by the research team. Results will be reported in the aggregate only. After both surveys have been completed, researchers will destroy all lists of participant names and e-mail addresses.

Questions? If you have questions about this survey, you may contact Julie Whitman, Director of Special Projects, at the National Center for Victims of Crime, 202-467-8741, jwhitman@ncvc.org.

If you are willing to participate, please click the **Continue** button below and follow the instructions. The survey should take about ten to fifteen minutes to complete.

What is your occupation?

- ○ Victim advocate
- ○ Prosecutor
- ○ Defense Attorney
- ○ Judge
- ○ Other [   ]

[for victim advocates] Where do you work?

- ○ Prosecutor's office
- ○ Police department
- ○ Community-based agency
- ○ Other [   ]

[for prosecutors] Which of the following types of crimes do you typically prosecute?

○ Felonies
○ Misdemeanors
○ Ordinance or code violations
○ Juvenile offenses
○ Other or more than one [   ]

[for defense attorneys] Are you a public defender or an attorney in private practice?
○ Public defender
○ Attorney in private practice
○ Other [   ]

[for defense attorneys] Which of the following types of crimes do you typically defend?

○ Felonies
○ Misdemeanors
○ Ordinance or code violations
○ Juvenile offenses
○ Other or more than one [   ]

[for judges] In which type of court do you preside?

○ District court
○ County court
○ Municipal court
○ Juvenile court
○ Family court
○ Civil court
○ Other [   ]

Please select **up to** three crimes you most commonly deal with in your work:

☐ Domestic Violence
☐ Sexual Assault
☐ Child Sexual Abuse
☐ Robbery
☐ Assault
☐ Homicide
☐ Drunk driving
☐ Property Crimes
☐ Other [   ]

Do You Agree or Disagree?

Indicate your level of agreement with each statement.

	Strongly Agree	Agree	Neutral	Disagree	Strongly Disagree
Crime victims should have explicit rights in the criminal justice process.	○	○	○	○	○
Crime victims should have legal standing to enforce their rights in court.	○	○	○	○	○
Crime victims should have the option of having an attorney represent them in criminal court.	○	○	○	○	○
There should be legal remedies for victims who are denied rights.	○	○	○	○	○

Indicate your level of agreement with each statement.

	Strongly Agree	Agree	Neutral	Disagree	Strongly Disagree
Victims' rights often conflict with defendants' rights.	○	○	○	○	○
My organization does not have sufficient staff to comply fully with victims' rights requirements.	○	○	○	○	○
Complying with victims' rights requirements frequently delays dispositions.	○	○	○	○	○
Victims' attorneys can be helpful to me.	○	○	○	○	○

Indicate your level of agreement with each statement.

	Strongly Agree	Agree	Neutral	Disagree	Strongly Disagree
Prosecutors in my jurisdiction comply with victims' rights requirements.	○	○	○	○	○
Prosecutors in my jurisdiction are willing to argue in court for victims' rights to be honored.	○	○	○	○	○
Defense attorneys in my jurisdiction accept crime victims' rights as written in Colorado law and do not actively oppose their exercise in the courtroom.	○	○	○	○	○
Judges in my jurisdiction are aware of and uphold victims' rights.	○	○	○	○	○

Please indicate how acceptable you would find each of the following potential remedies in the instance where a victim's right was clearly violated in a given proceeding.

	Always acceptable	Sometimes acceptable	Acceptable only in unusual circumstances	Never acceptable
New hearing on a plea agreement	○	○	○	○
New sentencing hearing	○	○	○	○
New trial	○	○	○	○
New parole hearing	○	○	○	○
Administrative sanctions for the violating party	○	○	○	○
Civil cause of action against the violating party	○	○	○	○

Victims' Rights Laws in Colorado—Test your knowledge

Under Colorado law, who does NOT qualify as a crime victim for purposes of exercising victims' rights?

- ○ The parent of a child sexual assault victim.
- ○ Victims of financial crimes, such as identity theft and fraud.
- ○ A robbery victim.
- ○ A murder victim's significant other.

- ○   A victim of vehicular assault.

The decision whether the victim provides written or oral input, or both, at sentencing is at the discretion of:

- ○   The court.
- ○   The prosecutor.
- ○   The victim.
- ○   The defense attorney.
- ○   The probation officer preparing the presentence investigation report.

Victims do NOT have the right to be informed of which of the following:

- ○   The decision not to file charges against a person accused of a crime.
- ○   The execution of an offender in a capital case.
- ○   Any subpoena for records relating to the victim's medical history, mental health, education, or victim's compensation.
- ○   A petition by their offender requesting expungement of juvenile court records.
- ○   The transfer, release, or escape of a person charged with or convicted of a crime from any state hospital.

Which one of the following statements about a victim's right to restitution under Colorado law is true:

- ○   An offender may not be ordered to pay restitution in one lump sum.
- ○   Victims are afforded the right to receive restitution under Colorado's crime victims' rights constitutional amendment, Colo. Const. Art. II, § 16a.
- ○   Restitution is required in every case where a crime victim has suffered pecuniary loss.
- ○   Restitution that is declined or unclaimed for two or more years after the final determination of a case is returned to the defendant.
- ○   Restitution may be ordered for physical or mental pain and suffering, loss of consortium, loss of enjoyment of life, loss of future earnings, or punitive damages.

Which of the following victim protections is an actual provision of Colorado law?

- ○   Victims are afforded a general right to be free from intimidation, harassment, or abuse.
- ○   A mandatory protection order restraining a person charged with a crime from harassing, intimidating, or retaliating against a victim or witness shall remain in effect from the time of arraignment or the person's first appearance before the court until final disposition of the case.
- ○   Law enforcement and prosecutors must provide reasonable efforts to minimize contact between the victim and the defendant, including providing a separate waiting area if possible.
- ○   An offender can be charged with the crimes of bribing a victim or witness, intimidating a victim or witness, aggravated intimidation of a victim or witness, retaliating against a victim or witness, or tampering with a victim or witness, all of which are class 3 or 4 felonies.
- ○   A victim of intimidation or retaliation may bring a civil action for damages.
- ○   All of the above.

Your Opinion

What changes would you make to your state's victims' rights laws and/or the way that they are currently being implemented?

Thank you!

Please contact jwhitman@ncvc.org if you have any questions regarding this survey, or call 202-467-8741.

Survey for Maryland, South Carolina, and Utah Criminal Justice Officials

This appendix reproduces the Survey of Criminal Justice Professionals on Victims' Rights.

Survey of Criminal Justice Professionals on Victims' RightsPurpose: The purpose of the survey is to gather information about the knowledge, attitudes, and behavior of criminal justice professionals with regard to crime victims' rights. The survey is part of a larger effort to evaluate the impact of crime victims' rights legal clinics in several states.Voluntary: Your participation in this survey is completely voluntary. You may leave any question blank and stop at any time. Your employment, affiliations, and standing in any group or association will in no way be affected by your participation or non-participation in the survey.Confidential: All survey responses are confidential, and your identity will never be revealed by the research team. Results will be reported in the aggregate only. After the survey has been completed, researchers will destroy any lists of participant names and/or e-mail addresses in their possession.Questions? If you have questions about this survey, you may contact Susan Howley, Public Policy Director at the National Center for Victims of Crime, 202-467-8722, showley@ncvc.org.If you are willing to participate, please click the Continue button below and follow the instructions. The survey should take about ten to fifteen minutes to complete.

What is your occupation?
❏ Victim Services Professional
❏ Prosecutor
❏ Defense Attorney
❏ Judge
❏ Other

Where do you work?
❏ Prosecutors office
❏ Police department or sheriffs office
❏ Community-based agency
❏ Other

Which of the following types of crimes do you typically prosecute?

Please contact showley@ncvc.org if you have any questions regarding this survey, or call 202-467-8722.

❑ Felonies
❑ Misdemeanors
❑ Ordinance or code violations
❑ Juvenile offenses
❑ Other or more than one

Are you a public defender or an attorney in private practice?
❑ Public defender
❑ Attorney in private practice
❑ Other

Which of the following types of crimes do you typically defend?
❑ Felonies
❑ Misdemeanors
❑ Ordinance or code violations
❑ Juvenile offenses
❑ Other or more than one

In which type of court do you preside?
❑ Circuit Court
❑ District Court
❑ Juvenile Court
❑ Appellate Court
❑ Other

Please contact showley@ncvc.org if you have any questions regarding this survey, or call 202-467-8722.

How many years have you been working in the criminal justice system in Maryland?

Do You Agree or Disagree? How Has Your Opinion Changed?

Please indicate your level of agreement with each statement in the left side of the matrix, then select the level of agreement in the right side of the matrix that best reflects what your opinion was six years ago (in 2004).

Level of Agreement Today[Strongly Agree, Agree, Neutral, Disagree, Strongly Disagree]

	1	2	3	4	5
Crime victims should have explicit rights in the criminal justice process.					
Crime victims should have explicit rights in the criminal justice process.					
Crime victims should have legal standing to enforce their rights in court.					
Crime victims should have legal standing to enforce their rights in court.					
Crime victims should have the option of having an attorney represent them in criminal court.					
Crime victims should have the					

Please contact showley@ncvc.org if you have any questions regarding this survey, or call 202-467-8722.

---

option of having an attorney represent them in criminal court.				
There should be legal remedies for victims who are denied rights.				
There should be legal remedies for victims who are denied rights.				

Please indicate your level of agreement with each statement in the left side of the matrix, then select the level of agreement in the right side of the matrix that best reflects what your opinion was six years ago (in 2004).

Level of Agreement Today[Strongly Agree, Agree, Neutral, Disagree, Strongly Disagree]

	1	2	3	4	5
Victims' rights often conflict with defendants' rights.					
Victims' rights often conflict with defendants' rights.					
My organization does not have sufficient staff to comply fully with victims' rights requirements.					
My organization does not have sufficient staff to comply fully with victims' rights requirements.					
Complying with victims' rights requirements frequently delays dispositions.					
Complying with victims' rights requirements frequently delays dispositions.					
Victims' attorneys can be helpful to me.					

Please contact showley@ncvc.org if you have any questions regarding this survey, or call 202-467-8722.

Victims' attorneys can be helpful to me.					

For each statement, please select the frequency with which it currently occurs on the left side of the matrix, then, on the right side, select your best estimate of the frequency with which it occurred six years ago (in 2004).

Frequency Today[Always, Usually, Sometimes, Rarely, Never]

	1	2	3	4	5
Prosecutors in my jurisdiction comply with victims' rights requirements.					
Prosecutors in my jurisdiction comply with victims' rights requirements.					
Prosecutors in my jurisdiction are willing to argue in court for victims rights to be honored.					
Prosecutors in my jurisdiction are willing to argue in court for victims rights to be honored.					
Defense attorneys in my jurisdiction accept crime victims' rights as written in Maryland law.					
Defense attorneys in my jurisdiction accept crime victims' rights as written in Maryland law.					
Judges in my jurisdiction are aware of and uphold victims' rights.					
Judges in my jurisdiction are aware of and uphold victims' rights.					

Please contact showley@ncvc.org if you have any questions regarding this survey, or call 202-467-8722.

_____
_____

Below is a list of potential remedies for violations of victims' rights, which may or may not be currently available. Assuming they were available, please indicate how acceptable you would find each remedy in the instance of a violation. Then, on the right side of the matrix, indicate how acceptable you would have found these remedies six years ago.

Level of Acceptance Today[Always acceptable when theres a violation, Acceptable in certain cases of violations, Never acceptable no matter the violation]

	1	2	3
New hearing on a plea agreement			
New hearing on a plea agreement			
New sentencing hearing			
New sentencing hearing			
New parole hearing			
New parole hearing			
Administrative sanctions for the violating party			
Administrative sanctions for the violating party			
Civil cause of action against the violating party			
Civil cause of action against the violating party			

What has changed?

Would you say that you know more about your state's victims' rights laws than you did six years ago?
❑ I know more
❑ I know less (my knowledge has gotten rusty)
❑ I know the same amount I did six years ago

_____

Please contact showley@ncvc.org if you have any questions regarding this survey, or call 202-467-8722.
_____

If your knowledge has increased, to what do you attribute your learning?

Have you had any contact with the Maryland Crime Victims Legal Advocacy Project or one of its attorneys? The attorneys include Russell Butler, Pauline Mandel, Jani Tillery, Lauren Tabackman, Bridgette Harwood, Catherine Chen, Gearald Jeandre, Melody Cooper, Joanna Oliver, Tracey Delaney and Sandy Bromley.

❏ Yes

❏ No

❏ Unsure

Please describe the nature of the contact.

If your contact was around a specific case or cases, do you feel that their involvement furthered the interest of the victim(s)?

❏ Yes

❏ No

❏ Unsure

On the whole, did their involvement further the interest of justice?

❏ Yes

❏ No

Please contact showley@ncvc.org if you have any questions regarding this survey, or call 202-467-8722.

❑   Unsure

How has your contact with the Maryland Crime Victims Legal Advocacy Project changed your view of victims rights?
❑   My view of victims rights is more favorable because of them
❑   My view of victims rights is less favorable because of them
❑   My contact with them did not change my view of victims rights

Thank you!

Please contact showley@ncvc.org if you have any questions regarding this survey, or call 202-467-8722.

---

1. Maryland Criminal Justice

Please contact showley@ncvc.org if you have any questions regarding this survey, or call 202-467-8722.

Survey for Victims

This appendix reproduces the victim survey.

Informed ConsentInstructions: Attempt to make contact as soon as possible after receiving the information from the screener, ideally within two to three days. Check to see whether best dates or times to call are noted on the intake sheet. Do not leave messages on answering machines.

When someone answers the phone:May I please speak with (NAME OF VICTIM)?

(If the respondent asks who you are):My name is (NAME) and I am calling about a survey on legal rights.

(If the victim is not available): Is there a good time that I could call back and reach (NAME OF VICTIM)?

Once the victim is on the phone:Hello, my name is (NAME) and I am with the National Center for Victims of Crime. Are you alone and in a place where it is safe for you to talk?

❑ Yes
❑ No

(If the victim says that she/he is alone in a safe place):I am calling to follow up on your recent conversation with (NAME OF SCREENER from PROSECUTOR/CLINIC)about participating in a research interview. Id like to explain to you what the interview is about and ask whether you want to participate. Can I go ahead?

❑ Yes
❑ No

(If the victim says yes):The interview is part of a federal study that is trying to help courts to assess whether crime victims are getting the rights they have under the law. I will ask you some questions about your satisfaction with the way you were treated by different people in the criminal justice system, the outcome of your case, whether you received the rights you are entitled to, and whether anyone helped you locate other services you may have needed. The interview should take between 15 and 20 minutes. It is 25 questions long, with the potential for a few follow-up questions. You will be paid $25 for your full participation and completion of the survey.The information you provide will remain strictly confidential. It will never be attached to your name or any other piece of information that could identify you. Your interview will be used in combination with interviews of other crime victims to form a picture of how victims are treated and whether their rights are respected in your state.Your participation is completely voluntary. You may stop the interview at any time, and you may refuse to answer any question. If you have to interrupt the interview for any reason but would like to complete it, we can arrange to call you back to finish the interview. If you need to stop for safety reasons and dont have time to schedule a call-back, simply say, I have to go, and hang up. We will attempt to call you back tomorrow to complete the interview. You can also call me back at 1-800-FYI-CALL. Thats 1-800-394-2255. Should I repeat the number?Do you have any questions?

Interviewer instructions:Answer all questions for which you have sufficient information. If there are questions you are unable to answer, refer victims to Susan Howley, director of public policy at the National Center for Victims of Crime, 202-467-8722. You may transfer directly to her extension from the Helpline, explaining to the victim that if Ms. Howley answers the phone, she will respond to their questions right away, and if the victim receives her voicemail, they should leave a message with their questions and the best, safest time for her to return the call.

Are you willing to go ahead with the interview?
❏   Yes
❏   No

Thank you for your time. If you change your mind or have any questions about the survey, or if you have needs related to the crime against you, you may call 1-800-FYI-CALL and ask for me, (INTERVIEWER NAME).

Can we do the interview now? It should take 15 to 20 minutes.
❏   Yes

❏ No

1. At any point after the crime was committed, were you given written or verbal notice of your rights as a crime victim?
❏ Written notice
❏ Oral notice
❏ Both
❏ Unsure
❏ No notice received

2. Who informed you of your rights?
❏ Police
❏ Prosecutor
❏ Victim advocate (prosecutor based)
❏ Victim advocate (police based)
❏ Victim advocate (community-based)
❏ Clinic staff
❏ Unsure
❏ Other

3. Was the defendant released from custody after arrest?
❏ Yes
❏ No
❏ Not sure

4. Were you notified of his/her release?
❏ Yes
❏ No
❏ Not sure

5. Who were you notified by?
❏ Prosecutor
❏ Victim advocate (prosecutor based)

❑ Victim advocate (police based)
❑ Victim advocate (community based)
❑ Clinic staff
❑ Jail/corrections
❑ Not sure
❑ Other

6. Were you asked at any point during the criminal case to turn over medical or other personal records to the defense?
❑ Yes
❑ No
❑ Not sure

7. Did anyone attempt to protect the privacy of those records for you?
❑ Yes
❑ No
❑ Not sure

8. Who attempted to protect the privacy of your records?
❑ Prosecutor
❑ Clinic attorney
❑ Victim advocate (prosecutor based)
❑ Victim advocate (police based)
❑ Victim advocate (community based)
❑ Judge
❑ Self
❑ Not sure
❑ Other

9. Was a plea offer made in your case?
❑ Yes
❑ No
❑ Not sure

10. Did the prosecutor consult with you before making the plea offer?
- ❑ Yes
- ❑ No
- ❑ Not sure

11. Were you notified of the sentencing date?
- ❑ Yes
- ❑ No
- ❑ Not sure

12. Were you provided with the opportunity to make a victim impact statement at sentencing?
- ❑ Yes
- ❑ No
- ❑ Not sure

13. Did you choose to make an oral statement, a written statement, both, or none?
- ❑ Oral only
- ❑ Oral, but had someone else deliver it
- ❑ Written only
- ❑ Both
- ❑ None

14. Did anyone help you prepare your statement(s)?
- ❑ Yes
- ❑ No
- ❑ Not sure

15. Who helped you prepare your witness statement?
- ❑ Prosecutor
- ❑ Victim advocate (prosecutor based)
- ❑ Victim advocate (police based)
- ❑ Victim advocate (community based)
- ❑ Clinic staff

❏ Not sure
❏ Other

16. Was there a conviction or guilty plea in your case?
❏ Yes
❏ No
❏ Not Sure

17. Were you notified of the conviction or guilty plea?
❏ Yes
❏ No
❏ Not sure

18. Who notified you?
❏ Prosecutor
❏ Victim advocate (prosecutor based)
❏ Victim advocate (police based)
❏ Victim advocate (community based)
❏ Clinic staff
❏ Not sure
❏ Other

19. Were you asked about crime-related losses for purposes of restitution?
❏ Yes
❏ No
❏ Not sure

20. Who collected that information from you?
❏ Prosecutor
❏ Victim advocate (prosecutor based)
❏ Victim advocate (police based)
❏ Victim advocate (community based)
❏ Clinic staff

❑   Not sure
❑   Other

21. Did the judge order restitution in your case?

❑   Yes
❑   No
❑   Not sure

For following questions, Im going to ask you to rate your satisfaction as extremely satisfied, satisfied, dissatisfied, or extremely dissatisfied(Interviewer note: 1=extremely satisfied, 4=extremely dissatisfied)

22. How satisfied were you with the way you were treated during the criminal justice process...

	1 (extremely satisfied)	2 (satisfied)	3 (dissatisfied)	4 (extremely dissatisfied)	N/A
By the prosecutor					
By the judge					
By the defense attorney					
By the prosecutors victim advocate (if any)					
By the clinic attorney (if any)					

23. How satisfied were you with the outcome of the criminal case?

	1 (extremely satisfied)	2 (satisfied)	3 (dissatisfied)	4 (extremely dissatisfied)
Outcome				

For the following questions, I'm going to ask you how strongly you agree or disagree with some statements. For these questions, you can strongly agree, agree, neither agree nor disagree, disagree, or strongly disagree. Let me repeat those options. . . (repeat)(Interviewer note: 1=strongly agree, 5=strongly disagree)

24.

	1 (strongly agree)	2 (agree)	3 (neutral)	4 (disagree)	5 (strongly disagree)
I felt I had the power to exercise my rights as a crime victim during the criminal justice process					
My rights as a crime victim were respected					
The criminal justice process was fair					

For the next part, I am going to read a list of needs that often arise for crime victims before, during, or after the criminal case. For each one, please indicate whether this need was something that applied to you or a close member of your family at any time between the commission of the crime and the end of the criminal case.

25. After the crime against you, did you or a close family member have a need for:

	Yes	No
Safe housing		
Financial assistance with expenses caused by the crime		
Medical treatment		
Counseling		
A support group		
Transportation		

Crime scene clean-up		
Protection from the defendant or his/her family or associates		
Another need that was caused by the crime		

For each need you indicated, I am now going to ask you whether anyone referred you to a resource that could meet that need

26. Safe Housing

Did anyone refer you to a shelter or safe housing program?
❏ Yes
❏ No
❏ Found it on my own
❏ Other

If yes, who referred you?
❏ Prosecutor
❏ Victim advocate (prosecutor based)
❏ Victim advocate (police based)
❏ Victim advocate (community based)
❏ Clinic staff
❏ Friend/word of mouth
❏ Other

Did you contact the shelter or program?
❏ Yes
❏ No

Was the need ultimately met?
❏ Yes
❏ No

❑ Ongoing

27. Financial assistance

Did anyone refer you to a resource for financial assistance?
❑ Yes
❑ No
❑ Found it on my own

If yes, who referred you?
❑ Prosecutor
❑ Victim advocate (prosecutor based)
❑ Victim advocate (police based)
❑ Victim advocate (community based)
❑ Clinic staff
❑ Friend/word of mouth
❑ Other

Did you contact the resource?
❑ Yes
❑ No

Was the need ultimately met?
❑ Yes
❑ No
❑ Ongoing

28. Medical treatment

Did anyone refer you to a medical facility or provider?
❑ Yes

❏ No

❏ Found it on my own

If yes, who referred you?

❏ Prosecutor

❏ Victim advocate (prosecutor based)

❏ Victim advocate (police based)

❏ Victim advocate (community based)

❏ Clinic staff

❏ Friend/word of mouth

❏ Other

Did you contact the facility or provider?

❏ Yes

❏ No

Was the need ultimately met?

❏ Yes

❏ No

❏ Ongoing

29. Counseling

Did anyone refer you to a counseling program or therapist?

❏ Yes

❏ No

❏ Found it on my own

If yes, who referred you?

❏ Prosecutor

❏ Victim advocate (prosecutor based)

❏ Victim advocate (police based)

❑   Victim advocate (community based)
❑   Clinic staff
❑   Friend/word of mouth
❑   Other

Did you contact the program or therapist?
❑   Yes
❑   No

Was the need ultimately met?
❑   Yes
❑   No
❑   Ongoing

30. Support group

Did anyone refer you to a support group?
❑   Yes
❑   No
❑   Found it on my own

If yes, who referred you?
❑   Prosecutor
❑   Victim advocate (prosecutor based)
❑   Victim advocate (police based)
❑   Victim advocate (community based)
❑   Clinic staff
❑   Friend/word of mouth
❑   Other

Did you contact the support group?
❑   Yes

❑ No

Was the need ultimately met?
❑ Yes
❑ No
❑ Ongoing

31. Transportation

Did anyone refer you to a transportation resource?
❑ Yes
❑ No
❑ Found it on my own

If yes, who referred you?
❑ Prosecutor
❑ Victim advocate (prosecutor based)
❑ Victim advocate (police based)
❑ Victim advocate (community based)
❑ Clinic staff
❑ Friend/word of mouth
❑ Other

Did you contact the resource?
❑ Yes
❑ No

Was the need ultimately met?
❑ Yes
❑ No
❑ Ongoing

32. Crime scene clean-up

Did anyone refer you to a resource for crime scene clean-up?
❏ Yes
❏ No
❏ Found it on my own

If yes, who referred you?
❏ Prosecutor
❏ Victim advocate (prosecutor based)
❏ Victim advocate (police based)
❏ Victim advocate (community based)
❏ Clinic staff
❏ Friend/word of mouth
❏ Other

Did you contact the resource?
❏ Yes
❏ No

Was the need ultimately met?
❏ Yes
❏ No
❏ Ongoing

33. Protection from the defendant or his/her family or associates

Did anyone refer you to a resource for obtaining a protective order or other type of protection?
❏ Yes
❏ No
❏ Found it on my own

If yes, who referred you?
- ❏ Prosecutor
- ❏ Victim advocate (prosecutor based)
- ❏ Victim advocate (police based)
- ❏ Victim advocate (community based)
- ❏ Clinic staff
- ❏ Friend/word of mouth
- ❏ Other

Did you contact the resource?
- ❏ Yes
- ❏ No

Was the need ultimately met?
- ❏ Yes
- ❏ No
- ❏ Ongoing

34. Other need (fill in from above)

Did anyone refer you to a resource for filling this need?
- ❏ Yes
- ❏ No
- ❏ Found it on my own

If yes, who referred you?
- ❏ Prosecutor
- ❏ Victim advocate (prosecutor based)
- ❏ Victim advocate (police based)
- ❏ Victim advocate (community based)
- ❏ Clinic staff
- ❏ Friend/word of mouth
- ❏ Other

Did you contact the resource?
❏ Yes
❏ No

Was the need ultimately met?
❏ Yes
❏ No
❏ Ongoing

35. Who or what was the most helpful to you during the criminal case?

[ ]

Thank you very much for completing the survey. The last thing I need to do is to get your address to mail you the $25 payment. I am going to take this information down in a separate place, and it will not be associated with the answers you just gave me. May I have the mailing address to send your payments to?

Advocate Name:

[ ]

Time spent:

[ ]

Case-File Data-Collection Form

This appendix reproduces the case-file data-collection form.

Docket #: _____   **Victim:** _____

Prosecutor: 1) Cache County   2) Salt Lake City   3) Salt Lake County

Sample: 1) Clinic case   2) Pre-clinic case   3) Post-clinic control

Rights observed:

____ Informed of rights

    ____ Right to be notified of court hearings

    ____ Right to express opinion on plea agreement

    ____ Right to submit VIS

    ____ Right to compensation

    ____ Right to restitution

    ____ Right to privacy

    ____ Right to protection

    ____ Right to speedy trial

____ Subscribed to VINE notification

____ Expressed opinion on plea agreement

____ Submitted VIS

___   Received assistance with compensation claim

___   Submit information on financial losses to court

___   Received restitution

___   Given information about victim services

___   Given referrals to victim services

___   Received victim services

References

Beloof, Douglas E., "Constitutional Implications of Crime Victims as Participants," *Cornell Law Review*, Vol. 88, No. 2, January 2003, pp. 282–305.

———, "The Third Wave of Crime Victims' Rights: Standing, Remedy, and Review," *Brigham Young University Law Review*, Vol. 2005, No. 2, 2005, pp. 256–370.

———, "Weighing Crime Victims' Interests in Judicially Crafted Criminal Procedure," *Catholic University Law Review*, Vol. 56, No. 4, Summer 2007, pp. 1135–1170.

Bibas, Stephanos, "Transparency and Participation in Criminal Procedure," *New York University Law Review*, Vol. 81, No. 3, June 2006, pp. 911–966.

Cassell, Paul G., "Recognizing Victims in the Federal Rules of Criminal Procedure: Proposed Amendments in Light of the Crime Victims' Rights Act," *Brigham Young University Law Review*, Vol. 2005, No. 4, 2005, pp. 835–926.

Davis, Robert C., James Anderson, Julie Whitman, and Susan Howley, *Finally Getting Victims Their Due: A Process Evaluation of the NCLVI Victims' Rights Clinics*, Washington, D.C.: U.S. Department of Justice, National Institute of Justice, August 29, 2009a. As of November 9, 2012:
https://www.ncjrs.gov/pdffiles1/nij/grants/228389.pdf

———, *Securing Rights for Victims: A Process Evaluation of the National Crime Victim Law Institute's Victims' Rights Clinics*, Santa Monica, Calif.: RAND Corporation, MG-930-NIJ, December 18, 2009b. As of November 9, 2012:
http://www.rand.org/pubs/monographs/MG930.html

Davis, Robert C., Nicole J. Henderson, and Caitilin Rabbitt, *Effects of State Victim Rights Legislation on Local Criminal Justice Systems*, New York: Vera Institute of Justice, February 1, 2002. As of November 13, 2012:
http://www.vera.org/content/effects-state-victim-rights-legislation-local-criminal-justice-systems

Davis, Robert C., and Carrie Mulford, "Victim Rights and New Remedies: Finally Getting Victims Their Due," *Journal of Contemporary Criminal Justice*, Vol. 24, No. 2, May 2008, pp. 198–208.

Earl, Jennifer, Andrew Martin, John D. McCarthy, and Sarah A. Soule, "The Use of Newspaper Data in the Study of Collective Action," *Annual Review of Sociology*, Vol. 30, August 2004, pp. 65–80.

Eikenberry, Ken, "Victims of Crime/Victims of Justice," *Wayne Law Review*, Vol. 34, No. 1, Fall 1987, pp. 29–50.

Englebrecht, Christine M., "The Struggle for 'Ownership of Conflict': An Exploration of Victim Participation and Voice in the Criminal Justice System," *Criminal Justice Review*, Vol. 36, March 2011, pp. 129–151.

Fritsch, Erik J., Tory J. Caeti, Peggy M. Tobolowsky, and Robert W. Taylor, "Police Referrals of Crime Victims to Compensation Sources: An Empirical Analysis of Attitudinal and Structural Impediments," *Police Quarterly*, Vol. 7, 2004, pp. 372–393.

Howley, Susan, and Carol Dorris, "Legal Rights for Crime Victims in the Criminal Justice System," in Robert C. Davis, Arthur J. Lurigio, and Susan Herman, eds., *Victims of Crime*, 3rd ed., Los Angeles, Calif.: Sage Publications, 2007, pp. 229–314.

Johnson, Ida M., and Etta F. Morgan, "Victim Impact Statements: Fairness to Defendants?" in Laura J. Moriarty, ed., *Controversies in Victimology*, 2nd ed., Cincinnati, Ohio: Anderson Publishing, 2008, pp. 115–131.

Kelly, Deborah P., and Edna Erez, "Victim Participation in the Criminal Justice System," in Robert C. Davis, Arthur J. Lurigio, and Wesley G. Skogan, eds., *Victims of Crime*, 2nd ed., Thousand Oaks, Calif.: Sage Publications, 1997, pp. 231–244.

Kilpatrick, Dean G., David Beatty, and Susan Smith Howley, *The Rights of Crime Victims: Does Legal Protection Make a Difference?* Washington, D.C.: U.S. Department of Justice, National Institute of Justice, December 1998. As of November 9, 2012:
https://www.ncjrs.gov/pdffiles/173839.pdf

Kilpatrick, Dean G., and Randy K. Otto, "Constitutionally Guaranteed Participation in Criminal Proceedings for Victims: Potential Effects on Psychological Functioning," *Wayne Law Review*, Vol. 34, No. 1, Fall 1987, pp. 7–28.

Lester, Marilyn, "Generating Newsworthiness: The Interpretive Construction of Public Events," *American Sociological Review*, Vol. 45, No. 6, December 1980, pp. 984–994.

Miller, Joel, Robert C. Davis, Nicole J. Henderson, John Markovic, and Christopher Ortiz, "Measuring Influences on Public Opinion of the Police Using Time-Series Data: Results of a Pilot Study," *Police Quarterly*, Vol. 8, No. 3, September 2005, pp. 394–401.

National Crime Victim Law Institute, "Mission and Values," undated. As of November 9, 2012:
http://law.lclark.edu/centers/national_crime_victim_law_institute/about_ncvli/mission_and_values/

———, *Crime Victims' Rights Enforcement Guide*, unpublished paper, 2009.

NCVLI—*See* National Crime Victim Law Institute.

Office of the Auditor General of Florida, *The Provision of Victim Services Pursuant to Section 960.001: Florida Statutes Operational Audit*, Tallahassee, Fla., 2001.

O'Hara, Erin Ann, "Victim Participation in the Criminal Process," *Journal of Law and Policy*, Vol. 13, No. 1, 2005, pp. 229–247.

Oliver, Pamela E., and Daniel J. Meyer, "How Events Enter the Public Sphere: Conflict, Location, and Sponsorship in Local Newspaper Coverage of Public Events," *American Journal of Sociology*, Vol. 105, No. 1, July 1999, pp. 38–87.

President's Task Force on Victims of Crime, *Final Report*, Washington, D.C., 1982.

Public Law 97-291, Victim and Witness Protection Act of 1982, October 12, 1982.

Public Law 98-473, Victims of Crime Act of 1984, October 12, 1984.

Public Law 101-647, Victims' Rights and Restitution Act of 1990, November 29, 1990.

Public Law 103-322, Violent Crime Control and Law Enforcement Act of 1994, September 13, 1994.

Public Law 108-405, Crime Victims' Rights Act of 2004, October 30, 2004.

Regional Research Institute for Human Services, Portland State University, *2002 Oregon Crime Victims' Needs Assessment: Final Report*, Salem, Ore.: Crime Victims' Assistance Section, Oregon Department of Justice, January 2003. As of November 21, 2012:
http://www.rri.pdx.edu/historic_projects_directory/crime_victims_directory/crimevictims_final_report.pdf

Ruback, R. Barry, and Martie P. Thompson, *Social and Psychological Consequences of Violent Victimization*, Thousand Oaks, Calif.: Sage Publications, 2001.

U.S. General Accounting Office, *Criminal Debt: Actions Still Needed to Address Deficiencies in Justice's Collection Processes*, Washington, D.C., GAO-04-338, March 2004. As of November 21, 2012:
http://purl.access.gpo.gov/GPO/LPS52016